The Glass Children

The Glass Children

Poems by Richard Cole

THE UNIVERSITY OF GEORGIA PRESS

ATHENS AND LONDON

© 1986 by Richard Cole
Published by the University of Georgia Press
Athens, Georgia 30602
All rights reserved

Designed by Betty P. McDaniel
Set in 10 on 13 Linotron 202 Meridien
The paper in this book meets the guidelines for
permanence and durability of the Committee on
Production Guidelines for Book Longevity of the
Council on Library Resources.

Printed in the United States of America

90 89 88 87 86   5 4 3 2 1

Library of Congress Cataloging in Publication Data

√ Cole, Richard.
    The glass children.

    I. Title.
PS3553.04733G53 1986   811'.54   86-4330
ISBN 0-8203-0872-2 (alk. paper)
ISBN 0-8203-0873-0 (pbk.: alk. paper)

The publication of this book is supported by a grant from the National Endowment for the Arts, a federal agency.

Acknowledgments

Grateful acknowledgment is made to the following
publications in which these poems first appeared:

The New Yorker: "The Last Days of Heaven"
Chicago Review: "The Pale Fish In Limestone Caves," "Muromachi
  Folding Screen"
Hudson Review: "Aubade," "Recovering In The Sandwich Islands"
Milkweed Chronicle: "Showing The Child I Have One Hand," "The
  Photographs of Carol Armitage"
TC Magazine: "The Glass Children"
Telescope: "In New York The Women Are Dreaming"

The author would also like to thank the Bush Foundation and the
Minnesota State Arts Board for grants which made it possible to
complete this book.

Contents

The Glass Children

The Illustrations of Andreas Vesalius

He takes a breath
And peels the compliant
Skin from the back of his hand
To show us clearly
The elastic engine of ligaments
And bone inside, the soft
Rein of tendons
Working the fingers.

It's high noon. He stands
Naked on a limestone ledge
Near Padua, assuming
A classic posture of Renaissance
Art, the broken viaducts
Stuttering across the valley
Behind him. We don't understand,
So he peels the skin back
Farther, revealing
The deep sympathy of flexor
With extensor muscle, layers
Rendered in logical sequence,
Intellect consuming the beautiful
Elements of the man by exact degrees,
As if blasted by surgeons.

So page by page we proceed
Without hesitation as the unbound
Body becomes articulate, skin
Billowing behind him like a tent.
"I am burning," I can hear him saying

Quietly like a lover, repeating the words.
"I am burning," and his body
Opens like a charm.

Baffin Island

All winter long we dreamed of food: tender,
Ineffable dreams of rump roasts

Simmering in their natural juices, potatoes
And baby carrots and hot berry pie. We dreamed

Of an English breakfast and the smell of bacon,
Biscuits broken open with honey

Drizzled over warm pats of butter melting
As we lifted our forks and woke up

Coughing in an open tent, in the Arctic, frozen.
It became a joke among us finally,

As, finally, it becomes impossible to calculate
Detachment at this latitude. Petersen now cries

When I cut away the useless skin from his toes,
More, I think, from the idea of it. If exploration

Is the "physical expression of an intellectual
Passion," then we are passionate

For the one idea and ourselves
At the center of it. I think of Scott,

Geologizing on Beardmore Glacier even at the end,
Turning a fragment of anthracite in his cracked

And deadened fingertips. "What appealed
Most strongly to me," he wrote,

"Was the suffering the Franklin had endured,
And a strange ambition burned inside me

To share that suffering." Petersen now shares
His letters to Frieda with me. Petersen

Is a woman. He lacks a relative understanding
Of the unessential heart. It is *not*

That I had more strength than the others
But only a greater hunger for success

So I burn, and Petersen dies. We have no choice
But to follow the offers of evolution.

Tomorrow I leave for the Pole, surviving
On the cold air if need be. I have never felt so

Utterly alone and happy. Washing my face
In the pool above Dexterity Bay, I rediscover

How the tender surface reforms,
Calm and perfect, aching to freeze.

4

Natural History in the Tropics

A bell rings in the forest
And early twilight
Enriches the colonial city.
Night blossoms open
And the street lights glow,
Turning their cups of light downward
On the late shoppers who hurry home.
In the marketplace, the merchants
Gather under strings
Of naked light bulbs, waiting
For village women
To hesitate over flowers
Stacked like cordwood,
Roots and tubers
Encrusted with earth,
Hard apples and sugar
Candy skulls from Mexico.
This is the hour
Of reception, a lamp
Shining in the open window,
And the heavy butcher
Steps out from his shop
And sets down a basin
Of organs floating in water
And pauses, watching the crowds,
His arms folded. In the open
Forest, however, the dark
Brown families are crawling awake,
Yawning, stretching their leather wings,
And they fly
By thousands into the night,

Maneuvering through the soft explosions
Of dahlia perfume where they feed
On the orange, passionate meat
Of papayas and mangoes. A flashbulb

Pops. For a moment we retain
An unconscious image
Of Gothic wings and pointed,
Rough tongues lapping the rind,
But by dawn the creatures have returned,
Fluttering back under the cool branches
As clusters of leather babies
Shudder. Mother is home.
The tender mouths unfold,
Oblivious, already searching
For the tiny pink.

Muromachi Folding Screen

To be conscious is to be
somewhere else.
—MERLEAU-PONTY

There, beneath an unconscious heaven,
Beneath a bony fretwork of crags

Floating half sunk on soft clouds
Covering and uncovering a world of mountains,

A merchant poles his grain boat
Past a nestled cottage where inside

A tiny woman with her drum is singing.
He raises his hand to call across

The evenly patterned water while overhead
Two thin lines of geese

Twist southward to another season
And do not suffer to notice

That for ten thousand years
She is never turning

To find at this moment
He is always passing.

The Pale Fish in Limestone Caves

Keep mainly to themselves, leading
The quiet life down there,
Free from distraction.

Full-grown, they are slightly larger
Than your little finger and hang
Silently in the pools, their icy fins

Barely feathering the clear water polished
Through so many miles of pure stone
It is almost not water.

And they have no stars, no vague seasons,
No light flooding the amazed chambers
Clustered with stalactites, rotting jewelry,

Roses, molars, staircases of wrinkled ivory
And sugar-pink, two-ton wedding cakes
Collapsing with a flurry of wings and centaurs

To disturb them so they are blind.
Their eyes rest like moist pearls
In their milky faces, and each creature

Will regard the other as a secret, gently,
As they reproduce with a pale shuddering
Their perfect lives.

Showing the Child I Have One Hand

I

Wonderingly, he
Touches the stump,
Gently maneuvers
The soft
Nubbin of a thumb,
Its baby
Nail.

This is hard, but I let him
Look as he wants, and he handles me
Considerately. I'm surprised
To remember
The first time I touched
The thigh of a woman,
My heart racing, reaching
The wetness inside her.
With the pure gaze of an animal,
He examines it, me, for a moment
Longer, still
Curious, as children are,
And I hold my breath,
Waiting for what he will say.
He rubs his nose and looks up.
"Does it hurt?" he asks.
"No," I tell him truthfully,
And he runs back to the other children,
Apparently satisfied.

I've been meaning to talk about this matter
In one way or another
For some time now, but like everyone else,
I suppose, I take myself too seriously.
Perhaps it comes with the condition,
Feeling that you're somehow inexpressibly
Special. So I want to tell you the story
Of Wittgenstein's older brother,
The second son in that brilliantly
Self-conscious family, a concert pianist
Who lost his right hand in the war,
Though he later commissioned Ravel
For a slower music to be played
With the one hand.

I see him sitting by himself,
Secure in the respectable family
Music room, perhaps like the one designed
By his passionately analytical brother,
Deliberate in every detail, almost severe.
We're in Vienna now. It's late afternoon:

"Do not be surprised," they had said.
His hand enters the music tentatively,
His one eye.
"Do not be surprised if repeatedly
You find yourself in your dreams
As if it were normal—we mean,
Before," and he thinks
This must be how the mind loses
Its body, how an empty room grows
Darker at the end of a day, the pale sky

Still shining at the windows, the brain
Sometimes taking years to decline
What is missing.

At the end of his sleeve, the phantom
Aches for an old perfection
That was never there,
Just as his last, inquiring note
Silvers into another you cannot hear.
You hear him now,
Touching the same, same chord
Over and over, searching
For the perfect end of the music
If only to show you that it doesn't
Really matter after all,
And that it does.

III

I remember how the brush trembled
As my father painted
Signboards for his business,
The wet, black tip
Hovering lightly above the panel
Until sinking at last
Into a long, sure stroke,
The Roman block letters
Emerging beautifully,
Balanced and square.
I once asked him—I was very small—
Why his hand shook when he painted.
For a moment he said nothing, vaguely
Irritated with the question, then said,

As if in compensation, "I'm afraid
Of making a mistake."

I want to have children.
I want to teach them, the way
My father, whom I love, taught me.
I take one of them in my lap,
A son perhaps, discovering noses,
Glasses, rediscovering one day
How his father is different.
I want this child
Who will ask me questions,
Who will ask, "Does it hurt?"
I could say something grave,
With implications
Left significantly unspoken,
But that's not what he's asking.
He's a child,
And he simply needs to know
If his father is hurt,
And I need to tell him
In all honesty, no.

Salisbury Cloisters in Bright Sunlight

Headstones ease back,
Dogging their owners home . . .

With a camera, I think of life
As a quiet priest, standing in an open doorway,
Watching the rain.

How much
Of the religious life
Is simply a daily attention
To detail? Holding my breath,

I focus on a frieze
Of tiny, white daisies
Surrounding the lawn.
Their bright yellow centers burn.
Everyone is asleep today.
The outer world becomes
Subdued, like distant thunder
In bones of the deaf.

Furnace Dream

We've been trying to make art
All night long. You're wearing
A white formal, as if for a prom,
And crying quietly to yourself
As we drive rapidly through the dark.
I'm too mad to talk.
In the back seat
There are three musicians
Dressed in white tie and tails,
Staring straight ahead
And sweating slightly
As they balance their black
Instrument cases on their laps.
Suddenly we come
To a huge iron furnace
Roaring at the end of the road,
Glowing orange, its doors
Swung open. I can feel the heat
On my face as we get out
And walk the last few feet.
Then we step into the fire, stumbling
Awkwardly across the cinders.
Inside, the roaring is so loud
We have to shout to each other.
I can't hear what you're saying,
And I kneel down,
Hypnotized by the liquid
Shimmer of the fire, watching
The flames drip from my fingers,
And I only wake up
To find you

Turning away with a look
Of fading forgiveness,
The musicians now
Struggling to open their cases.
Tearing at locks,
Their fingers burning,
Their sharp screams becoming
Airy, ever fainter.

Recovering in the Sandwich Islands

Gentlemen, it was during my late fever
That I noticed the entire Unitarian compound

Reduced to the pure forms of geometry: irradiant
Rooftops and parallelograms still faintly tinged

In purple like the halos on the bloodless orchids
That amaze me every morning. I've found

That there's nothing to fear, that thought
Is a passion like everything else, and yet

In my conversations with Mr. Kalanimoku,
I cannot tell him exactly where passion leads.

It is his wife, I think, that leads a procession
On the anniversary of their reluctant lord's death.

Outside my bedroom window, a New England whaleboat
Sails down Water Street on the faithful shoulders

Of twenty retainers. In it, the fat queen sits,
And, gentlemen, she cannot help but be beautiful,

Though she looks through the men beneath her
As if they were blind.

Something has been lost, says Mr. Kalanimoku,
And thinking I understood, I told him

The story of Jacob: "I shall not let thee go,"
But he only looked farther away, at the ocean,

Slowly crushing a rope of hibiscus
Like tissue, and he is right.

I will never find in his words that "anguish
Which marks our true conversion,"

But I will teach the children the laws
Of true proportion and symmetry, their faces

So intent with intelligence becoming human
That you finally understand how beautiful they are

With a feeling torn slowly out by the roots
Of an enormous sadness, though you don't feel sad.

The Glass Children

Our children seem indestructible at times,
Racing through the iron playground with energy
That's almost frightening, and then

It happens. My son falls. I hear the tiny finger
Snap like cold taffy, and slowly a crystalline tear
Rises at the corner of his eye. I know he's ashamed,

And I hold him, smoothing his hair, wanting to explain
That for years his mother and I had tried so hard
For flesh and blood, but I can't.

Each year they grow stronger, slowly learning
How brilliant their bodies are, how easily
Broken. Each year, they become more graceful,

But my youngest daughter still tugs at my sleeve,
Telling me something in glass, and she sounds
Like someone rubbing a wine glass until it sings

Even as she tries to speak, each word ascending
Helplessly into perfect tones,
And she cries when I can't understand her.

At night my wife and I lie awake, talking quietly
About the children, about ourselves, and she asks
If I still want her. I squeeze her hand,

And I wonder if we'll always have the faith to make
More love. I wonder if the love we've made
Will always be glass.

Aubade

Between one dream and another
The grave eyes open, and morning clouds

Slowly gather together their bright bones.
The house still ticks with sleep.

All night, there were giants in another country.
The minute I move, they stop and turn

White with listening. Years from now
They may reemerge, blinking in daylight,

Shrunken with honor, with old relations
Of topaz and blind fish, but today

I lie here awake, watching you sleep.
The sky rises toward heaven.

Three oranges rest normally
In a china bowl.

Bad Poems

I wrote bad poems. One after another.
They would gather on my front porch
Like stunted children, their wet mouths

Pressed against the screen door as they tried
To see what I was doing. I would sigh.
I would throw down my pencil

And grab them by the hair, twisting it, hard.
When I sat down to work in the morning
They were gone. "To become a poet," I read,

"You must first be a butcher," so I am.
I can tell you exactly what I want from a poem,
But I can't tell why these have returned.

For the past three nights, I have seen them
Suddenly standing on the well-trimmed edge
Of the driveway as if they were waiting.

I step outside. Instantly they break away
Like deer and pause to look back
With a sad, new understanding in their eyes

That frightens me. They're wild now
And will not desert me, like all the bad poems
I never wrote.

Natural Progressions

I keep returning to study
The misshapen
Baby shoes, the plastic
Leg, a set
Of aluminum fingertips
Hanging in the window display
Of the Minneapolis Artificial Limb
And Brace Company, fascinated
Not by what I am, Mother,
But by what I could allow myself
To become: a cool device
Terminated in a hook. I'm bewildered
When I think of the enormous hatred
I feel at times, the unformed anger
And I look at myself again, as if
For the first time, wondering
If I were born with a part of my heart
Missing, just as a part of my body
Is missing. How human
Can I be? I ask myself.
And even now I hold myself
Apart, telling you this
With only the greatest of labor,
Reluctant and proud.

We say nothing but the obvious
To one another, year after year.
I can see an embryo
Suspended in clear fluid,
Unbreathing, soft, blind, covered
With a pale shroud of tissue

Like an old man raising
A shawl up over his head.
I remember how the complicated love
Flickered across your face for a moment
As we tried to say goodbye
At the airport terminal. I said
Nothing, and you looked so pretty
For your hesitance, like a girl
As I turned away, your silent,
Untouchable son.

Why do the men who write poetry have
So little to say about their mothers,
Or have we been talking all these years
Of nothing else?
I've never been able to leave you
The only way I can, by returning
Your gift. I only have a part
Of myself to offer, these still
Unfinished lines, an embryo straining
In the darkness beneath the heart, beginning
Its natural progression, the slow,
Involuntary growth of love.

An Aquarium in California

They rise
Trembling to the surface,
Beautiful and devouring
The soft cake
Of shrimp: angels and butterflies
Furiously nudging one another
For the pink flecks of meat, and this
Is California. I'm drinking
And watching the aquarium life,
Half-reading a Selective Criticism
Of American Lit as the Golden Gate
Appropriately dissolves
Into a monumental Pacific fog.

Looking back, I can see now
I was alcoholic, though it didn't
Seem to matter then. Some days
Were almost perfect, and the years went by.
Inside me, there's a hairy man with a knife,
Bug-eyed and savage. The moment I relax,
He starts to shake. I don't breathe,
And he seems so furious, almost desperate
When I don't fight back, that it frightens me.
But by drinking, I can move underwater,
Beneath him, enormous and reserved.
Granted he's only a picture in my mind,
But it helps me understand.

As I drank, I would watch the aquarium
Organize itself. The fish were wild,
First generation, with no place

To escape the order they made
With one another. I once released
A Harlequin Red into the tank,
Plump as a puppy and bearing
A soft train of rufflelike fins.
Excited, the others closed in,
Testing, pushing him back,
Until suddenly, too fast to react,
They reached a decision
And jerked out the gills,
Vigorously chewing
The fins down to boney
Stubs and left him, tumbling on the gravel,
The trim, blue damsels returning occasionally
To nudge, to peck a little at the body.

In the life of the mind, the world becomes
Connected, and hence more real, I thought.
I remember myself standing beside a bed
The morning after, still shaking a little.
She was sick and miserable with herself, rocking
From side to side on the pillow with tears.
"Please help us, Richard. Help us, help us, please,"
And I, looking down at her body, her back
Arching under the sheer nightgown, the long curtains
Billowing in the ocean wind.

In the end, there was only Grover left,
My lionfish, magnificent and sullen.
He would only eat
Live food, so I fed him goldfish,
And he glared, feeling the fresh body
Shudder in the saline water.
Slowly his spider fins splayed open,
Undulating with expectation

As he drifted closer, burning, obsessed,
The spring inside him winding
Tighter and tighter until finally
He approached to within an inch
Of the fish's head
And in one instantaneous convulsion
Sucked in a huge slug of water
And that was that.
The goldfish was gone, vanished, a few
Tiny scales swirling where he'd been,
And only a moment later did you notice
The last of the golden tail
Peeking out from between Grover's lips.

Why am I telling you all this?
I'd like to say that somewhere
In California something was lost.
I'm sober now, leading a life of limits,
Or trying to, on a frozen lake in Minnesota.
I try to construct an image of all those years
When we tried to be characters
In a wonderfully bad movie. Here I am,
Calling up old friends at night—
"Jack," I ask, "what was the meaning
Of our life out there. Does freedom
Invariably entail a sense of loss,
And what about love?" He says he doesn't know
And to call again. But nothing was lost.
I know that even on the clearest nights
I can still see those hot, exotic colors
Swimming freely in their small, bright cell
And myself on the island of California,
The sun always shining, the mornings
Cool and unbewildered.

The Telephone at the End of the Mind

I listen to the sound
Of water gently
Reasoning its way
Through limestone
Underground, and I think
Of another world
Dissolving endlessly
Into the earth. I think
Of the knock
And chuckle of bone
Melting into milky lacework,
Milk hardening into bone,
And I follow
The odd chambers for miles,
Adjusting to the cold
And dark, exploring
The beautiful geometry
Of rock broken and reformed
By the heavy government of water.
Even here, there are forms
Of life slowly evolving,
The tiny, urgent heart needing
Less and less to survive until finally

The telephone rings.
I pick it up. No one is there,
But all night I lie awake listening
To the sound of the ocean and somewhere
The wind blowing across the receiver.

The Last Days of Heaven

I see so many of us
Wandering down to the unmoving end
Of an ocean pier
At dawn, after the party,
The men in their yellow uniforms,
The ladies in brushed silk. The sea is calm.
Overhead, the Japanese lanterns sway
Simply in the breeze, their blue
Green pastel lights
Still burning, and we pause, all of us,
Looking up for a moment
At the clouds, clouds upon clouds
Building across the eastern sky, and we hear
Huge, distant voices calling to one another
Like faint music, the sound rising and falling on the wind,
A few notes, sometimes a phrase,
Then nothing . . .

I believe in conclusions, in a final
Whiteness absorbing the unequal
Flesh, our lives
Turning beautifully away
From the dim, reductive beasts
Inside us. I remember
The lion, the enormous peacocks
Bristling on the palace lawn, and the ox
Raging, wild-eyed, swinging the beard of wolves
Hanging at his throat, desire
Frozen in a moment of blood and speed,
And the moment fades, effective and resolved.

I believe we're approaching the essence
Of pure idea, all the lost energies of the world
Released formally in the mind. It becomes
A kind of grieving at last,
The beginning of peace as we congregate
In our brilliant white rooms, cool
And exhausted, like angels starving on sugar.

The Photographs of Carol Armitage

Such is the photograph. It cannot
say what it lets us see.

        —BARTHES

PREFACE

When I stand at the brilliant edge of the roof,
There is always the man who continues forward

Without hesitation, slipping smoothly out of my skin
And I'm lost, watching the back of his head,

His strong arms spreading open as he steps
Soundlessly over the edge.

*　*　*

"I want to be objective. At the same time, the severe
Nature of Carol's story will impede a purely
Clinical detachment. She was born in 1939,
Grew up in Connecticut and attended Radcliffe,
On scholarship, graduating with high honors in 1958.
In the spring of 1959, she admitted herself

To Brightlawn, complaining of chronic insomnia.
I began seeing her in March. From the very beginning,
I felt a disturbing respect for this woman. She possessed
Enormous integrity, and, despite her final actions,
A kind of unthinking bravery we find difficult to admit
Is lacking in ourselves. My first desire

Was to romanticize her story and my own, but this impulse
Was rebuked by her very nature: acerbic, quietly ironic,

29

With birdlike movements, not delicate, more like a hawk
With large, staring eyes. As our discussions progressed,
She resisted most direct questions, but slowly I began to see
Connections between her brief, spontaneous writings.

She was writing a play, she told me, though what I saw
Was a confusion of quotes and private images suggested
From early daguerreotypes. She became obsessed
With the pictures, telling me they illustrated her work.
My notes are therefore intended only as reference
Rather than as paraphrase or final explanation."

PART ONE

At first there is nothing
And then, as if rising
Innocently to the surface of milk,
The intangible
Details of the plant
Emerge: vulval slits and interstices,
The blind seed and phalli, tiny bracts
And the soft charms of trumpet vine
Extended like magic, a breathless
Clarity as the lines grow
Stronger and intelligent and rare.

It is probably the "automatic"
Nature of photography
That allows us to think
Of Objectivity, though
Whatever is captured
By the camera is deformed,
If by nothing else,

Than by the specific nature
Of the lens used.
But the last thing I want
Is "self-
Expression" smeared between
Myself and the field of vision.
I could live
In a world of images alone,
Perfect and complete.
Outside my window, I see
The almost sickening
Blur of the elm trees swaying
Blindly in the wind. Objects
Mock me, impenetrable,
But the photograph enters the mind
With immaculate detail, toothy
Edges of a leaf, tendrils
Engraved with a realism you can
Almost touch.

*   *   *

"Her appearance is faultless, even severe, but her room
Is a growing welter of books, negatives, prints, etc.
She sits in the center, the outline of her 'play'
Scotchtaped around the walls, photographs filling
Gaps in the scenario. She smokes constantly. This is the result,
I'm afraid, of running a 'modern facility.' Still,

She seems happiest when working alone, repeatedly revising
Her early drafts. She shows a greater reluctance now
To answer my questions, but looking at her work,
I see glimpses of herself between the actions

Of the various characters, like the unspoken history
Between the portraits of a family album."

* * *

But the play begins
And ends with the fall
Of sunlight on the Easter lawn,
The gentle intelligence
Of shadows that lie
Broken across the laps
Of three young women.
They are sisters, resting
In the late afternoon.
The wind moves the trees overhead.
In the house, someone
Lights a lamp in the parlor
Window. I can see
Each perfectly razored gesture
Held in the idle conversation, their
Momentary smiles, and the worried expression
Of the youngest, waiting for their father.
No one moves. They have lived
All their lives in the still, unbeating
Heart of the country, far from the ocean.
The fiction is growing, but the more
I step back to study this perfect
Illusion of a world, the more
I have the freedom to believe in the soft
Lace at their throats, the wicker
Pattern in the basket at their feet,
And I know: these are the images
The blind would see, if they could
In their dark light, her hand

Forever raised in the atmosphere
Of another century.

*   *   *

"She becomes even more self-contained, and shows
Greater difficulty with expression. I realize now
That she lives in an almost totally optical
Reality. I see her standing hesitant at the window
Tracing what she sees on the glass. She gasps
Like a fish, as if unable to breathe. My questions

Have no effect. She has periods, however,
Of unnerving clarity, and she tries to explain
The 'crystalline perfection' she wants, but fails
To finish the thought. Today, she describes her mind
As 'the funhouse, a modern tunnel
Of reflections receding between two mirrors.' "

*   *   *

His eyes stare through stone, through a moment
of twilight in the Victorian studio.

And his ivory cane, the horn buttons on his vest,
His iron sleeve laid on frosted marble,

Emerge precisely from a sleeping balance
Of blindness and an old idea of light.

The plate is exposed twice, however, a second figure
Ghosting the first, a young woman,

Transparent and persistent, her eyes
Striking you like two clear pieces of glass

With tiny lights behind them. The figures share only
This intimately bewildered design,

Both of them still joined
Obscurely at the waist, both leaning forward

As each attempts to escape into shadow
Beyond the other. This is the way

It should be, the old parlor where they sit
Preserved in a deep hypnosis of detail,

As if light were a drug, steady and remote,
As if you were staring down over the edge

Into the heady water of the reservoir,
Your shadow wavering on the bright sand below,

The water plants uncoiling their green intelligence
Thoughtfully to the surface.

PART TWO

"After almost a year, she suddenly began
Displaying moments of anger, for no apparent cause.
When I casually mentioned that she must be enjoying
The warm hydrotherapy baths, she immediately
Flinched, 'I *don't* enjoy them. You know that.
I'm here to be productive, to make progress, not loaf

Like these other slugs. You *make* me waste time here.'
And then a furious outburst, as if from nowhere:
'I'm *filth*! A little filthy piece of white disgust!'
The next morning, much calmer, she appeared

34

In bright orange pajamas, with two heavy bruises
On her cheekbones, which she would not discuss."

* * *

He was captured by the sea,
Angelicus Domenicus, called Angel
Protéstant, green and savage.
He will be a European man, I think,
Though he says he comes from China
Where he led his little nation
Into war. I see him in the second act
Standing naked by the cliffs,
Naked and furious,
Scrambling down the rocky shingle
As our party approaches,
And he turns at the edge,
Clutching his wounded head,
The Roaring Boy, stuttering:
'DON'T KILL—KILL ME!'
But more from anger than fear,
More a command—red-faced.
Oh, he was passionate!
And we bound him hand and foot
As he hissed through his hair,
The villagers jumping back,
Which always evoked some
Burst of immoderate
Though friendly laughter
From the orderly staff.

I have great regard for this man,
Though he barely articulates
The simplest ideas, as if partially
Paralyzed. I know he is miserable,

I can see the enormous pressure
In his face as he answers
The slightest question,
Each word laboriously uttered,
As someone put it, 'like rocks
Splitting,' the spittle fairly
Exploding off his lips. I can say
At this point, however,
That his wound has successfully
Hardened to a firm scar forming
A curious, gutter-shaped slit,
Tapered at both ends
As if cut with a gouge
Through the left parietal, its
Opening not being observed
To pulsate, that being
Tough and somewhat
Cool to the touch.

*   *   *

"She has a well-calibrated tendency to shock: 'thick
Ropes of blood slapping the hardwood floors,' and
So forth coming from her pen. But she remains
Silent when I question her meaning. The appearance
Of this new character, the 'savage man,'
Seems out of place with the preceding sections,

But he shows far more energy than earlier work, itself
A promising sign. Taking my cue, I suggested
That 'Angel' might need care from both of us.
'What would you do if I took a lover?' she asks,
As if changing the subject. I can only reply that a stronger
Sense of self is needed before entering into relationships."

*   *   *

The definitude with which
I approach this boy
Is scarcely counterbalanced
By the surging fantasies
He chooses to create. I know
That if left alone he becomes
Lost among the horses, petting,
Stroking their manes. He speaks
Only to them, confiding
His lordship
In another hemisphere.
Here he commands what he can.
I saw him once
Being bathed by the women
On the lawn, and suddenly
He rises in the wooden tub
Still manacled, the suds
Sliding slowly down his body,
And it was late in the evening
When they led him in . . .

Last night I discovered him
Squatting naked in his cell, staring
Up at me from under his shaved
And blistered skull, and he lunged,
His mouth yawning just
As the Mary door slammed shut.
Over and over, I felt
The steady "whump" of his shoulder,
More powerful from being
Restrained, his full
Weight shaking the oak,

And I thought to myself
"I'm safe" as I held it
With all my strength.

* * *

"Daily she becomes more of a perfectionist, more
Removed in her little world. She avoids the other patients,
Especially the men. Appears nervous, abrupt.
She also seems physically irritated with herself.
When I mention a fine tremor in her hands,
She dismisses it with only the vaguest distaste."

* * *

Outdoor luncheon.
Staff. 1892.

The men stare
Profoundly at the camera,
Mustaches soaked in beer,
Aware of themselves as forming
A memorial to mental healing,
Their precious food
Half-raised to their lips,
Their lips half-opened forever
As the urgent summer around them
Bristles and dies.

And if these figures move, they move
Like heavy jewels, dense
And growing under enormous
Pressure, the sunlight

Warming the bone
China a woman
Unconsciously holds
In her hand. This woman,

However, becomes the image
We remember, the youngest daughter
Waiting for her father.
She ignores the remote fingers
Of ivy plucking at her skirt, details
Raging in the grass
Beneath her and sits
To one side, as if being
Punished. Yet we can see
Such quiet irony
In her eyes, as if she knew
Already that at this moment
The world stands like crystal

And she is drowning. There.
The camera clicks just
As she starts to speak and
Everyone turns away smiling,
Once more in the rapid world,
Their mouths yawning open,
Laughing, their already
Furious gestures
Accelerating into light.

PART THREE

We have autumn now, season
Of the pure mind. Already I see myself

Released and walking through Boston Commons,
The white ash dividing and subdividing

Their branches in the cold, still air,
Each twig stiff with intellect. There are days

Now when everything shines with an aching
Clarity, the leaves swirling in wild patterns

That astonish me. 'So what is logic?' he asked,
Smiling at his students, as men will do,

Smiling at their students, and I thought,
'Logic is the iron branches of a tree

Infecting the mind, branches in the water . . .'
All my life I have lived beside the point,

But I stagger awake, the dreams pouring out of me
Like water, the images growing sharper. I see

Myself driving through heavy traffic, my arms
Aching for the long moment of impact,

The passionate head flung forward and back,
The car doors opening like wings and I'm

Floating in the mother arms of the accident,
Blood pounding, brilliantly alive.

*   *   *

"She seems convinced she's leaving, although it's obvious
Her condition grows worse. She now possesses
Some new-found energy. Even tries to approach

The other patients, who seem bewildered. I take
Her to one side, tell her she needs to stay.
Suddenly, she begins to cry, saying, 'God, I feel

So *lonely* at times. I can barely breathe.
And I haven't done a thing!' She seemed
On the edge of panic. 'What do you
Have to do?' I asked. Then, patiently,
As if talking to someone from another country,
Another species, she said, 'There is a part

Of us that isn't—how would you say?—humane?'
'I know,' I said, 'and we can help you
Heal that.' She looked up with her swollen
Eyes, carefully blew her nose, then said,
'Don't patronize me, you son of a bitch,'
Even with a hint of pride, and walked out."

*   *   *

As my name is Angel, I once
Held the face of my youngest
Minister, almost a child,
By the eyesockets. I remember
He screamed like a girl
As his vacant, milky expression
Burst like reluctant berries
Across my snow white sleeves.
Instantly I was silent: their lord,
And they led him waving through the garden,
Blind as water . . .

Today I see nothing but white,
And white excites the imagination,
As though in triumph.

Examine me, doctor.
See where the scalp
Is sheared away, the blinding
Side of my skull. You can see
The white thought logic, besieged
And surging through the wonder net
Of glassy veins, and my jaw is clenched.

At night, I have watched heat lightning
Flickering in the thunderheads
Dark flash, dark clouds,
And the other side of my brain is dark.
Brain cut in two. The single
Hemisphere—I cannot
Reach you, precious woman.
And I see myself surrounded
By your crystal image. I cannot
Touch you and roar, smashing
Every image of your face, birds
Exploding from the startled heart.

*   *   *

"It was at this time that she began to lock herself
In the bathroom, emerging a short time later,
Bleeding from the mouth. 'I couldn't help
Taking them out,' she insisted, and continued
Until nine teeth were left, which became infected
And had to be removed. I prescribed a low dosage

Of Mellaril, then Librium. She complained
Of an unidentified pain in her fingers and
Convulsively fractured the small bones, first
Of her left hand, then of her right, using

The bedsprings to help accomplish this.
All other attempts at medication failed,

And we moved her to the Med II ward. That night,
The nurse on her rounds discovered her kneeling
In bed, holding her left eye loosely in her palm.
She appeared to be mentally clear,
And certainly she became more reasonable
Than she had been for years."

*   *   *

I imagine some
Tiny insect horror
Quietly implanting
Its eggs under my skin
And I listen to the nurses
At their station who listen
To Johnny Mathis on the radio.
'This is real,' I think,
'This is really happening.'
And I touch the tiny
Holes at the corner
Of my mouth. I feel
Nothing, rubbing the dull
Lump on my arm, and I think
Of my skin tightening, swollen,
Until finally it breaks open,
The larvae crawling. I think
Of myself screaming, trying
To claw the arm away from me
And I see my chest rising,
Cracking open like a melon
And gently the huge white

Wings emerge, 'And my name
Is Angel,' he says,
'Gasping and beautiful,
Strong arms
Already extended, one
Perfect foot already uplifted
Until there's nothing but white as I rise
Above you, remarkable and free.'

*   *   *

"Horrific as they were, these final actions produced
A new-found calm in Carol, as if she had proven herself
Immune to outside, human attempts to help her,
And so could begin to heal. I knew
She had made whatever bargains were necessary,
Though I wondered what she thought she ever owed."

*   *   *

I remember the blue
Ascending peace

Those last few mornings, waking
To one bright voice,

Then another, showing them my badges
Of courage with a human happiness

That could only be human.
Outside, I hear iron children play

In the world among the trees, now
Farther and farther away. A door

44

Shuts in the mind. Then another,
And scarlet maples brilliantly turn

To the smell of woodsmoke in the evening.
The end now feels like a beginning.

All up and down the panic ward, the patients
Are grinning, becoming angels.

CONCLUSION

"Carol's work remains unfinished. She now lives
In another state, married, with two children,
A boy and a girl, I believe. She continues
To write. I haven't seen her in over a year,
And yet I still feel the lack of a formal
Resolution, although her recovery was rapid.

My last question was whether I could honestly say
That my work had helped her. 'I used to feel,'
She wrote, 'that I had to *justify* myself,
That my images had to be on the very edge of "saying
Something," though now I realize, even with a kind
Of relief, there was nothing that had to be said.' "

* * *

I was the landlord who ate their flesh.
Like deer, they came to me every morning, and
Somehow I can't remember their faces, only
A lip, an eye twisting toward the ceiling. I remember
Their childish energy at first, the laughter
And excitement in the crowded hallways. You

Probably think like a yellow animal
I savaged them into pieces,
Sucked them down whole,
Still alive and trembling and
Fresh like crisp celery, and, true, it *was*
Sexual in those days, though nobody knew it then,
And even now the warm wind carries the flags,
Yellow silk, then yellow and white,
Out patiently to their tips and falls.

At night, I listen to the bells in the wind,
I listen for my own soft pet
Who wanders in her bare feet
Through the halls at night, a tiny
Bell around her throat,
But I only see the child, confused,
Lost in the red haze, his arms
Spreading open as he slowly
Steps forward, calling my name,
His eyes as large as summer
But darker now—I try to understand—
As his love grows bewildered
And gradual and human.

In New York the Women Are Dreaming

In New York, yes, the women are dreaming,
In the lacework of hallways, hesitant with pearls,
In the violets of evening, from one night to the next,
In the amber water of Victorian aquariums,
Alone, under glass in the Hotel of Stars,
The women are dreaming and beginning to dream.

And in cold steel driving Manhattan, the women are
    dreaming,
In marble and granite, in the city's hunger
And the food that feeds it, in the energy
Enforced on its aging body, dying and expanding,
The women are dreaming and beginning to dream.
They're dreaming in the long weight of the physical buildings,
In masculine iron weeping in the walls,
Dreaming in concrete, in the crumbling legs
Of the elevated trains, in the trains going over,
In the freeways and archaic bridges,
The women are dreaming and gathering the dreams.

They're dreaming in boilers buried underground,
In untouchable voltage, in the warm relays,
In the cool face of computers, silent, thoughtless,
In precise twinklings of magnetic data,
In green waves of traffic surging by minutes,
In crowds climbing from the burning subways,
In the wondering child half-carried up the steps,
Looking up, the sunlight on his face,
In the summer rain, falling feverishly, straight down
And filling the streets with the sound of water.

They're dreaming in money, in the glittering,
Delicate conduits of trust
Surrounding the world, in desire,
In platinum ingots stacked in freezers,
In the severed heads floating through the hallways
Of the mild, organic corporations,
The women are dreaming and returning their dreams.

In the hands of the butcher the women are dreaming,
In the delicate reasoning of fat, in the carcass
Draining, lightening, in the broad, clean breasts
And flying shoulders, in the moist sawdust of bone
And teeth, in trotters, in the milk of the vein
Split open, in the tongues of cattle
Swung loose and pendulous, organs of the earth,
Of the lamb, of the life we feed on,
The women are dreaming.

In the broken body, in the frozen nerve
Of the doctors, the women are dreaming.
In the snowy white rooms, in the shoulders of men
Bending over the patient, in scalpel and response,
In needle, in clamp, in blood
Foraging through gauze, under drugs and asleep,
In Bentatrax, in Tri-barbs and Nidar,
In the lost collection of Quaaludes and Valium,
In Placidyl, in Lotusate and Seconal and Largon
And under the government of Thorazine,
The women are dreaming and trying to dream.

In the shoes of the dead the women are dreaming,
In Death's double song, in the coffins of men
And the coffins of women, the women are dreaming,
Fitful and stubborn, the buildings burning
All night in the Bronx, in Manhattan and Brooklyn.

They're dreaming in the neon smeared on the asphalt,
In screaming hallways, in iron cold darkness,
In twelve men taking turns
In a vacant lot, fires burning in the steel drums.
In the brain of the rapist, the women are dreaming
And dreaming to breathe.

The women are dreaming at sea, underwater,
In the dark hulls of ships steaming in moonlight
Toward harbor, in planes and buses approaching the city,
In the rhythms of railroads.
They're dreaming in Central Park at dawn,
In the streetlights still burning, in the lovers
Coming home, dreaming as he takes off his shirt
And kneels, kissing her legs and belly, so carefully,
Sliding his hands up under her dress, loosening
The fabric and she draws him up, and with them
The women are dreaming and almost awake.

They're dreaming in the bright wreckage of God
And a Goddess burning, dreaming the dawn
As they stand on the towers of Manhattan,
Patient, their free, white dresses
Floating in the wind, and their eyes are open
And they're dreaming of a world returning and alive,
Dreaming of the world and dreaming of women.

The Contemporary Poetry Series

EDITED BY PAUL ZIMMER

The Contemporary Poetry Series

EDITED BY BIN RAMKE

J. T. Barbarese, *Under the Blue Moon*
Richard Cole, *The Glass Children*
Wayne Dodd, *Sometimes Music Rises*
Gary Margolis, *Falling Awake*
Aleda Shirley, *Chinese Architecture*
Terese Svoboda, *All Aberration*

YOUNG, *UNDERSTANDING THE NEW TESTAMENT*

AN INTRODUCTION
TO THE NEW TESTAMENT

Books by
Edward W. Bauman
Published by The Westminster Press

An Introduction to the New Testament
The Life and Teaching of Jesus
Intercessory Prayer

AN INTRODUCTION
TO THE
NEW TESTAMENT

by

Edward W. Bauman

THE WESTMINSTER PRESS
Philadelphia

For

Deborah
Kathleen
and
Mark

"Thanks be to God through
Jesus Christ our Lord!"
— *Rom. 7:25*

Contents

Preface

THE NEW TESTAMENT is the fundamental document of the Christian faith. From the beginning, it has been the primary source of inspiration and authority for Christians who call themselves "the people of a Book." How strange it is, therefore, to discover so few of the people actually reading the Book!

There are many reasons for the lack of familiarity with the New Testament, which is characteristic of modern Christianity. Written in an ancient language in an ancient time, its voices seem distant and unreal. Reading progress is slow because our eyes stumble over unfamiliar words, archaic ideas, and paragraphs that have been mercilessly cut into verses. Footnotes or "chain references" disrupt the flow of ideas. Separated from the occasion that brought them to light, forced into an awkward format, our present documents might raise problems even for Peter and Paul!

Still more serious is the lack of coherence and order in the present arrangement of the New Testament books. There are twenty-seven of them, actually a small library, but they do not appear in chronological order, nor are they grouped according to style or purpose. Many are so obviously written to meet specific situations that readers

without sufficient background are apt to feel quite left out
of things. In view of all these difficulties, how can modern
Christians hope to read the New Testament with under-
standing? Too many of us feel like the Ethiopian who was
reading Isaiah when Philip ran up and asked him, "Do
you understand what you are reading?" He replied in dis-
may, "How can I, unless someone guides me?"

Most readers need a guide, a book that will "introduce"
them to each of the New Testament writings, setting them
in chronological order and answering the pertinent ques-
tions that suggest themselves to any thoughtful person.
Who wrote the book? When? Where? And above all, why?
There are countless introductions available that seek to
answer these questions, but many of them fall short at two
crucial points.

In the first place, few authors emphasize the factor that
accounts for the basic unity of the New Testament writ-
ings. There has been too much stress on the variety of
New Testament religion and the diversity of thought and
expression. Such variety and diversity are all too obvious.
There is no plot or story line, as one interpreter remarks.
But there is one basic theme that holds all the books to-
gether — the good news of what God has done in Jesus
Christ. All the writers have experienced in some authentic
way the Christ-event, all are eager to share it with others.
Their lives have been transformed because of the recon-
ciliation with God that Christ made possible. Inevitable
variety appears when they begin to describe and interpret
God's act in Christ, but "an introduction to the New Testa-
ment" should never lose sight of the basic experience that
gives a sense of unity and coherence to the whole.

In the second place, many New Testament introductions
do not meet the needs of their readers because they are
too detailed and abstruse. This field demands increasing

specialization on the part of scholars, a continual "speaking in tongues" in search of new truth. Unfortunately, not many of the "specialists" take time to interpret their findings for the nonspecialist. This does not mean that an introduction needs to be watered down to a level below that of the intelligent reader. It does mean that key facts and conclusions must be lifted out of the maze of technical detail that is necessary for the scholar but not for most readers. In this present volume an attempt has been made to present the "heart of the matter" in a clear and orderly way.

The book has been designed to meet the needs of individuals and groups. It will be used, along with the New Testament, as the textbook for college-level television courses throughout the country, but its use is by no means confined to this purpose. Any individual or group may use the material as an introduction to the text of the New Testament and as a guide for individual inquiry and group discussion. Questions and suggestions have been included in the appendix to stimulate study.

Introductions to the books, which have been placed in approximate chronological order, are presented in three stages: (1) The *background* will be examined so that the writing can be seen in the context of the occasion that brought it to life. Determining the author, date, purpose, occasion, and content of each document is the principal task of a New Testament "introduction." (2) One or two of the most serious *problems* not covered in the background discussion will be outlined for further consideration. Economies of time and space do not permit us to plunge deeply into the science of New Testament criticism, but familiarity with some of the major issues will enrich our understanding. (3) An *outline* of the book's basic contents will conclude each chapter. Some readers may wish to purchase an inexpensive edition of the New Testament and inscribe these outlines in the margin of the individual documents to facilitate reading and study.

Concluding with an outline leaves the reader "up in the air," but this has been done for a definite purpose. Too many Bible courses and too many books about the Bible never get around to the Bible text. An introduction to the New Testament is never an end in itself. It should never leave the reader feeling satisfied. On the contrary, it should whet his appetite for the pleasures of reading and "rightly handling" the word of truth in the original documents. The success or failure of any introduction can be measured by the degree to which it succeeds in achieving this purpose.

Every phase of this book, from preface to appendix, has been fashioned with this end in mind. The attempt has been made to point the way to the New Testament, which points, in turn, to the Christ.

EDWARD W. BAUMAN

Washington, D. C.

Chapter 1

God's Good News

THE NEW TESTAMENT is the most important book ever written, because it is a record of the most incredible good news in human experience. Those who first heard it found their lives utterly transformed. Many who had been filled with fear and anxiety discovered a peace beyond all understanding. Others who had been unable to discern any purpose in life suddenly possessed the one thing needful. Hungry hearts were filled to overflowing with the good things of God's own life. The lame arose and leaped for joy. The blind were made to see God, the deaf to hear his voice. They shouted and sang and preached and prayed, covering the known world with the news of what God had done for them, and their contagious joy broke into the stagnant life of the ancient world like a fresh breeze blowing into a musty room. Because of this event, human existence had become fully meaningful. Man's long journey into night had become a journey into light.

It is impossible to understand the New Testament if we separate it from this atmosphere of holy joy, high drama, and great excitement. Too many persons approach these books as if they were entering the dusty halls of an ancient historical museum, but such an approach misses the whole point of what the New Testament writers were trying to do. All of them were simply describing and interpreting something wonderful *that had happened to them:* God's coming into their midst in the person of Jesus Christ.

This Christ-event is so profound that no one can fully sound its depths. Yet it is at the same time profoundly simple. The Holy God who had been revealing himself in partial ways to men of old suddenly revealed himself fully. He who had not left himself without witness among any people was now fully reflected in the face of Christ Jesus, and because of his coming, men who had formerly been estranged from God were reconciled to him and entered into a new life of love. They became new creatures, new beings, new men and women "in Christ."

This full revelation of God, so unexpected and overwhelming, was recorded in the twenty-seven books that make up our New Testament. The true nature and unity of all these documents can be grasped only in the light of the experience that brought them to life.

Contrary to much popular opinion, for example, the New Testament did not give rise to Christianity. On the contrary, these writings emerged from a Christian movement that was vigorous before anyone thought of writing books and letters about it. The early Christians first had a common experience — God's mighty redemptive act in Jesus Christ. Those who had this experience were quite naturally drawn together into a common fellowship. At first they had little interest in written records of what was happening to them. Gradually, situations arose that called forth letters and books, but always to meet some particular need, to serve some particular purpose. Because they were written to meet the needs of a particular occasion, the New Testament documents are often called "occasional writings."

We can now readily see why it would be difficult, if not

impossible, to understand these documents apart from the
situation that called them forth. Only when we know the
conditions in the Corinthian church, for example, can we
comprehend what Paul is eagerly trying to tell his friends
there. Not until we feel the terrible danger in which the
Roman Christians were living, can we understand why
Mark is in such a hurry to get to the story of Jesus' suf-
fering and death. So it goes for every one of the New
Testament writings. One of the main purposes of any com-
petent New Testament introduction must be the re-crea-
tion of the actual situations that called forth the various
books.

The early Christian experience of God's mighty act in
Christ also accounts for the basic unity of the New Testa-
ment. A first serious reading of the twenty-seven writings
usually leaves us with a feeling of chaos and confusion
rather than of coherence and order. The authors have run
the full scale of human thought and emotion, each using
his own particular style in trying to meet the immediate
situation that he confronted. Most obvious and serious is
the wide variety of doctrinal interpretation, ranging all the
way from the conservative and legalistic emphasis of Jew-
ish Christianity to the Hellenistic (Greek) tendencies in
the Johannine writings; from the religion of Paul, with its
theme of faith, to the moralistic preaching of James; from
the priestly interests of Hebrews to the otherworldly vi-
sions of The Revelation. In view of such diversity it is diffi-
cult to speak of "New Testament belief" or of the "New
Testament point of view."

In the midst of all this diversity, however, there is a
basic unity in the common experience that brought the
early Christians together in fellowship and led them to
write letters and books. All agreed that God had somehow
spoken a definitive word through Jesus Christ. All agreed

that God had acted in Christ to make it possible for men to be reconciled to him in newness of life. When it came to describing and clarifying the meaning of the experience, they followed separate paths, but this is not surprising, since these writers represent the widest possible variety of national and cultural backgrounds. Yet they were bound together in their common experience of God in Christ. Those who do not keep this in mind will soon be discouraged by the New Testament's apparent lack of coherence. The experience held them together even while their interpretation of the experience tended to lead them apart.

One of the lingering recollections I have of Bethlehem at Christmas is a memory of such unity amidst diversity. Pilgrims come to Bethlehem at Christmas from all over the world. The little public square in Bethlehem in front of the magnificent old Church of the Nativity looks like a meeting place for the United Nations — Europeans, British, Americans, Asiatics, Africans, all met together in a perfect babel of tongues! Coming from such divergent backgrounds, those of us who had journeyed to Bethlehem for the Christmas season had little in common beyond our common experience of God's act in Jesus Christ. But this was enough! A strange feeling of unity bound us all together as we joined in the celebration of the birth of the Christ. Soon after Christmas we departed on our separate ways, but I will never forget the unity of experience that I felt binding us together in spite of our great diversity.

It is this same feeling which pervades the New Testament from beginning to end, from Matthew's stately Nativity story to the closing visions of the New Jerusalem in The Revelation. These men have all experienced God's mighty act in Christ, so they all have good news to proclaim. Proclaim it they do, in a wide variety of ways, but the good news is the tie that binds them all together in a great unity of exultant praise and thanksgiving. "Thanks be to God, who gives us the victory through our Lord Jesus Christ."

This unity of experience is evident at every stage of the New Testament writings. Consider the earliest Christian message as reflected in the sermons recorded in the book of The Acts (Acts, chs. 2 to 13). After an opening recognition that Old Testament prophecy is now fulfilled, Peter and Paul both proceed to give a brief account of the life, teaching, death, and resurrection of Jesus. Each interprets this Christ-event briefly, ending with an appeal for repentance and faith in the forgiving love of God now available through Jesus Christ. This is apparently the earliest form of the evangel, or good news.

In his writings, Paul proclaims the same gospel even though the letters do not represent systematic preaching or teaching. On the contrary, they are primarily defenses of his gospel against misunderstanding and attacks from his opponents, but in the give-and-take of debate we can discern the essential form of his message. He had been set free from obedience to the law by Jesus Christ and had entered into a new life of reconciliation and love. This is the theme that he talks about in such exalted terms and defends so vigorously.

The gospel in the Gospels is equally apparent, as Mark's opening words make quite clear: "The beginning of the gospel of Jesus Christ." John tells us that "these things are written that you may believe that Jesus is the Christ, the Son of God, and that believing you may have life in his name" (John 20:31). It is not without reason that the books themselves are called Gospels, or "good news."

Evidence of this same common experience may be found in all the other writings, as will be seen when we examine them in detail. The important point here is that the New

Testament is a unity in this most basic sense, for it arose out of a common historical experience. This common experience was God's act in Jesus Christ, which they felt as a life-transforming surprise and which they described as incredible good news.

Our plan of study in the following chapters will lead us into the widest possible variety of situations in our attempt to reconstruct the occasions that gave rise to the various documents. We will encounter great diversity of style and form, nor can we escape the great divergence of interpretation and "point of view" that is apparent in the emerging doctrinal disputes of the early church. But if we can remember through it all the common experience of the Christ-event out of which the diversity emerges, we will not be too confused and dazzled by the kaleidoscope that revolves around us.

The profound simplicity of the New Testament is grounded in a historical event, God's mighty act in Jesus Christ. This act is the good news, the "tidings of great joy" for all people.

Chapter 2

First Thessalonians

1. Background

THE EARLIEST Christian document we possess is a letter from Paul to some of his friends. Anxious about their welfare, he had just received good news from them that prompted him to tell them of his gratitude and continuing concern. He wrote to them in Thessalonica from the city of Corinth about the year A.D. 51. How strange that the written records of the Christian faith begin in such an informal and intensely human way!

Saul of Tarsus had been a strict Jew, educated in the city of Jerusalem and zealous beyond all imagination to obey the sacred law. But he found no peace until the day he was confronted by a vision of Christ that so completely transformed his life that he changed his name to symbolize his "new birth." Saul, the Pharisee, became Paul, the Christian. No longer the estrangement from God; no longer the frustration of fruitless attempts to achieve salvation through obedience to the law; no longer the disappointment of crying aloud to God only to hear the echo of his own voice. Paul, the well-intentioned, restless prodigal, had been welcomed home!

Supreme among the changes in Paul's life was his new attitude toward Jesus of Nazareth. Prior to his conversion, he had looked upon Jesus as a false messiah and upon his followers as blasphemers. He had been a leader in the persecution of Christians, headed for Damascus with orders to persecute them, when the "light from heaven" broke upon him. From this moment he lived "in Christ," absolutely certain that Jesus was Messiah, Savior, and Lord.

Our examination of Paul's writings will reveal more clearly the nature of this experience, but we must emphasize here that all the letters are a direct result of his transforming encounter with Christ. He simply could not stop telling about what had happened to him, nor could he stop talking about the God who made it possible. His enthusiasm led him into a life of travel that took him all over the Mediterranean world. Wherever men would listen, Jew or Gentile, slave or free, he proclaimed the good news of what God had done in Christ for him and for all men. Suffering unbelievable hardship on account of this gospel, he was beaten, stoned, shipwrecked, lost, "on frequent journeys, in danger from rivers, danger from robbers, danger from my own people, danger from Gentiles, danger in the city, danger in the wilderness, danger at sea, danger from false brethren; in toil and hardship, through many a sleepless night, in hunger and thirst, often without food, in cold and exposure." Through it all, he was driven relentlessly to share with all men the riches of Christ. If the word "apostle" means "one sent with a message," no figure in history deserves the title more than Paul!

During his many travels, which had taken him from Asia Minor into Europe, he had founded churches in the chief cities along the way, bringing together into fellowship those who shared the experience of God in Christ. One of his first stops in Asia was the Greek city of Thessalonica, the chief seaport and capital city of Macedonia, whose location on the military highway to Rome gave it unusual strategic importance. Paul began his mission here by preaching on three successive Sabbaths in the Jewish synagogue, but he soon turned away from the Jews when he discovered the pagan population listening with greater eagerness to his message. In this way, the church in Thessalonica came to be made up primarily of new converts from paganism, partly explaining why Paul wrote in such elementary terms to his friends there. He took his stand on a few simple fundamentals of the faith, because the Thessalonians had no Old Testament foundation on which to build.

His mission in Thessalonica was unfortunately cut short by the hostility of some Jews who provoked a riot against him. Forced to leave quite suddenly, Paul journeyed on to Athens and then to Corinth. His labors in both places demanded all his attention, but he could not forget the Thessalonian Christians, struggling to find their way as "babes in Christ." Would they be overcome by enemies of "the word"? Growing increasingly anxious about them, he sent Timothy, one of his most trusted companions, to express his concern and inquire about their welfare. When Timothy returned with good news, Paul hastened to write a letter expressing joy and thankfulness. The specific *purpose* of First Thessalonians is (*a*) to express warm personal affection for his friends and (*b*) to offer words of practical instruction on matters of the Christian faith that had been brought to his attention.

The mood of joy and thanksgiving dominates the letter. "We give thanks to God always for you. . . . And we also thank God constantly for this. . . . For what is our hope or joy or crown of boasting before our Lord Jesus at his coming? Is it not you? For you are our glory and joy. . . . For what thanksgiving can we render to God for you, for all the joy which we feel for your sake before our God?" Here is an excellent example of the intensely warm and personal character of Paul's letters, and an example, too, of the strong relationship that Paul built up with his converts. Here was no hit-and-run evangelist, but a man who had merged his life with those whom he brought to Christ.

In his practical instruction to these new Christians, Paul had two main concerns. First, he wanted to impress upon them the necessity for moral purity in the Christian life, and especially in their attitude toward relations between the sexes. In nearly every city where a church was founded, Paul ran into the easygoing pagan attitude on this subject. Since it turns up as a problem in several of his letters, we should not be too surprised to find it here in this first letter to the Christians of the Greek city of Thessalonica. He emphasizes that those who have found God in Christ are eager to follow the will of God, hence they abstain from all immorality and uncleanness in their personal relationships. Among Christians, he insists, marriage is honored and respected as sacred.

His second concern is with those who misunderstood his teaching concerning the Second Coming of Christ. Paul had told them that the Christ who had risen from the dead and ascended into heaven would soon return to earth to inaugurate God's Kingdom. Those who were still living would witness this glorious event and enter into eternal life with their Lord. But the Thessalonians were now wondering about their friends and loved ones who had already died. Had they missed the opportunity to share in the experience of Christ's coming again? Paul answers with words of comfort. Those who are dead in Christ will rise first in order to be ready to meet the Lord at his coming.

We have no way of knowing when this will be, except that it will probably be when least expected, like a thief in the night. The Christian is therefore vigilant and always ready for that great day when the living and the dead in Christ will enter into the glory of his coming.

2. *Problems*

There are relatively few serious problems involved in the study of First Thessalonians. Since the chronology of the New Testament documents is always complicated, however, we should note here the way in which dates are often established. Cross references among the New Testament writings are used whenever possible and these are checked against other contemporary records. A reference in The Acts, for example, tells us that a Roman proconsul named Gallio arrived in Corinth near the end of Paul's year and a half stay in that city (Acts 18:12–17). A fragment of a letter written by Emperor Claudius, recently unearthed at Delphi, tells us that Gallio was proconsul of Greece from approximately A.D. 51–52. Thus if Paul wrote First Thessalonians very soon after his arrival in Corinth, he must have written it about A.D. 50–51. It is extremely helpful to be able to date the earliest New Testament writing with such a degree of accuracy.

It is also important to note Paul's final request, "that this letter be read to all the brethren." This helps us see that he prepared his messages for a rather wide audience. In another place (Col. 4:16) he even directs neighboring churches to exchange his letters. Since extra copies would probably have been made for this purpose, we may have here an indication of why many of his letters have been preserved. They were not dashed off in thoughtless haste, but were prepared with studied concern for the problems of the early Christians who very early made extra copies of them. The sustained argument in some of the later epistles is evidence of the profound thought lavished by Paul upon his writing. Apparently somewhat deficient in his ability as a preacher ("I did not come proclaiming to you the testimony of God in lofty words"), he more than made up for this weakness in his matchless correspondence.

3. Outline

1. Salutation (ch. 1:1)
2. Personal concern for the Thessalonians (chs. 1:2 to 3:13)
   a. Joy and thanksgiving (ch. 1:2–10)
   b. Defense of himself against his opponents (ch. 2:1–16)
   c. Explanation of his failure to return (chs. 2:17 to 3:13)
3. Words of instruction (chs. 4:1 to 5:22)
   a. Warning against immorality (ch. 4:1–12)
   b. Instruction concerning the return of the Lord (chs. 4:13 to 5:11)
   c. General instructions (ch. 5:12–22)
4. Conclusion (ch. 5:23–28)

Chapter 3

Second Thessalonians

1. Background

THE MOOD and contents of Second Thessalonians make it quite clear that Paul's earlier letter had been seriously misunderstood. He had counseled his friends to wait for the coming of Jesus with patience and steadfastness of faith. No one knows the day of the Lord's coming, he had taught, but we must be ready, for it will come suddenly, when we least expect it. The Thessalonians, interpreting "suddenly" to mean "immediately," unfortunately fell into difficulties that often plague those who become excited about the end of history (eschatology).

When men believe that "the end" is at hand, they may lose interest in their daily work and in other normal responsibilities. Why labor to produce goods and earn wages that will soon be worthless? This is apparently what had happened to some members of the church in Thessalonica, who stopped working and were living at the expense of their fellow Christians. Such a practice was unfair to the members who continued to labor, and it gave Christianity a bad name among the heathen, encouraging the idea that Christians were fanatics who became idlers and busybodies.

Paul, concerned about the possibility of such a misunderstanding, had forewarned his friends in his earlier letter, urging them "to aspire to live quietly, to mind your own affairs, and to work with your hands, as we charged you; so that you may command the respect of outsiders, and be dependent on nobody" (I Thess. 4:11–12). But they had not heeded his warning and so he wrote again from the city of Corinth very shortly after the first letter (A.D. 50–51). His *purpose* is (*a*) to explain more precisely what he had said about the coming of the Lord and (*b*) to correct abuses that had arisen because of misunderstanding.

"Now concerning the coming of our Lord Jesus Christ"— this is Paul's main concern, and his words about the Second Coming represent both a modification and a development of that which he had previously written. Paul was firmly convinced that Jesus was the Messiah, but he had also learned from the Old Testament prophets that the Messiah would come in judgment and initiate the Day of the Lord. Since Jesus had not performed this function, Paul was certain that he would come again. But now he warns the Thessalonians that this cannot happen until an antichrist appears to bring the sin of the world to its climax (II Thess. 2:1–12). This Antichrist, whom Paul calls the son of perdition or the "man of lawlessness," will claim divinity for himself and lead the powers of evil in a mighty rebellion against God. Now held in restraint, he is building up his forces, and when the restraining power is overcome he will unleash his terrible power. For a time he will seem to triumph, but at the height of his power, "the Lord Jesus will slay him with the breath of his mouth and destroy him by his appearing and his coming" (II Thess. 2:8).

This idea of an antichrist or devil's messiah arose in early Jewish eschatology and appears several times in the New

Testament (Mark 13:14; Matt. 24:15; I John 2:18; 4:3).
It was believed that Satan would gather up all of his power
and make one last attack when he perceived that the King-
dom of God was imminent. Evil would become incarnate,
seek men's allegiance by signs and wonders, and establish
a kingdom of sin and lawlessness. In the book of The Reve-
lation the Antichrist plays a central role, but there is a
striking difference between The Revelation and Second
Thessalonians. In the former, Antichrist is Rome, whereas
in his letter Paul insists that Rome is the restraining power
holding back the "son of perdition." But soon the restrain-
ing power will fall, and the "son of perdition" will be
released. All of this, Paul insists, must take place before
Jesus will return.

Modern readers find this passage confusing at best, re-
pugnant at worst. Most Christians have moved beyond this
type of fanciful apocalyptic prediction and speculation.
But behind the language and thought forms, which seem
strange to us, there is an important concept. The "spirit of
lawlessness," lurking beneath the surface, waiting for the
restraining power to be removed, seems all too real at
times. Periods of great social and political turmoil often
give ample evidence of evil breaking forth when law and
order are overthrown. Sometimes the evil is so great it
seems to be the very opposite of all the goodness and love
in Christ — hence the Antichrist. This truth is back of
Paul's words, though the majority of persons today are not
expecting the drama to unfold as Paul describes it. Paul,
in fact, greatly modified his own position in his later letters.

Furthermore, the great apostle had absolutely no pa-
tience with the abuse of his teaching by those who gave
up their work and lived in idleness. Throughout his entire
ministry Paul insisted on supporting himself by work out-
side of his preaching. He was a tentmaker, a worker in
leather and animal skins, who practiced his trade in every

city where he settled for any length of time. The preaching of the gospel took place only in the hours left "after work." In view of this attitude, we can understand Paul's anger at the idlers in Thessalonica. In his letter he reminds them of the example that he had set and pleads with them to get back to work and earn their own living. At this point he establishes a vital standard for church life: "If any one will not work, let him not eat" (II Thess. 3:10). Those who disobey are to be excluded from the fellowship of Christians.

Undoubtedly one of the more important passages in Paul's letters, this statement is one of the earliest attempts to establish the principle that honest work is an integral part of Christian discipleship. The Kingdom of God is still the one thing needful in man's life, but this does not exclude daily labor for the necessities of life. On the contrary, the highest expression of religion is that which relates itself to every area of life, particularly an area as important as work. This teaching had a profound influence on the church, especially in the Reformation doctrine of the sacredness of man's vocation or "calling."

2. Problems

Many scholars think it impossible that Paul wrote Second Thessalonians. They cannot believe that the man whose great religious teaching has come down to us in other documents could be the author of the fanciful apocalyptic speculation that is at the heart of this letter. According to this view, Second Thessalonians is a revision of the first letter by a later hand. When the Lord did not appear in the next generation, one of Paul's followers revised his first epistle in order to explain the delay in the great event that Paul so confidently expected. In the process of revision, many of the apostle's ideas were retained, but the central passage (II Thess. 2:1–12) was added and cannot be attributed to Paul. In support of this view, interpreters emphasize that a man like Paul, so full of original and creative ideas, would not have written two letters so similar in content to the same people.

Such arguments are not convincing. It is easy to see how a second letter was called forth by the misunderstanding of his teaching in the first. Things like this happen frequently in correspondence between persons. Moreover, in writing again so soon after the first letter, Paul might repeat phrases and ideas that were still uppermost in his mind. We also know that there was an apocalyptic tendency in his thought that manifested itself from time to time (cf. I Cor. 2:6). On the other hand, there are too many of Paul's characteristics in this second letter to view it as an imitation or even revision. It is vigorous in mood, logical in form, and rooted in the immediate situation that Paul faced as he tried to lead his Thessalonian friends closer to God through Christ. We may therefore accept the Pauline authorship of Second Thessalonians in spite of objections that have been raised.

3. *Outline*

1. Personal greetings (ch. 1)
   a. Salutation (ch. 1:1–2)
   b. Thanksgiving (ch. 1:3–12)
2. The coming of the Lord (ch. 2:1–12)
3. Words of comfort and instruction (chs. 2:13 to 3:18)
   a. Exhortation to faithfulness (chs. 2:13 to 3:5)
   b. The problem of idleness (ch. 3:6–12)
   c. Benediction and farewell (ch. 3:13–18)

Chapter 4

Galatians

1. Background

GALATIANS, one of the primary documents of religious history, might well be called the Christian Declaration of Independence. When it was written, a serious threat to the Christian movement had sprung up, led by teachers from the church in Jerusalem who were visiting churches everywhere with a fantastic claim: Gentiles must first become Jews before they could become Christians! Paul opposed this "false" teaching so violently and so eloquently in this Galatian letter that it has served for nearly two thousand years as the basic document of Christian freedom.

Equally significant is the description of the fundamentals of Christian faith that Paul uses as the foundation of his argument. "What does it mean to be a Christian?" Few persons can answer this question intelligently, but Paul leaves no doubt about the matter here. In defending his gospel, he gives a clear, vigorous, and unmistakable statement of the essence of the Christian religion. It is not by accident that many revivals of religious faith, including the Protestant Reformation, have been deeply rooted in

Galatians. Certainly the coming reformation of the church, so desperately needed, will have to pay attention to this unparalleled book.

There has been a great deal of dispute among scholars as to the precise location of the Galatian churches. The name Galatia properly referred to a region in the north of Asia Minor, but Paul uses the term to designate the cities along the southern coast, Antioch, Iconium, Lystra, and Derbe. There were churches in each of these cities founded by Paul and Barnabas on their first missionary journey into the area. Because they were among his earliest converts, Paul felt especially close to these Christians, visiting them whenever possible, rejoicing in their faith. Here also, in the church at Lystra, he found the faithful Timothy.

We can imagine, therefore, the deep sense of shock and grief that the sensitive apostle must have felt when he heard of the serious trouble in these churches. The news came to him during the early part of his stay in Ephesus, probably about the year A.D. 54. Eloquent and persuasive "Christian" teachers from Jerusalem had appeared in these churches, attacking Paul's authority and denying the validity of his gospel. Paul, they claimed, was no true apostle at all. He had not been one of the Twelve, nor was he authorized to offer his own interpretation of the gospel to the pagans. By so doing, he was misleading them and thus imperiling their souls and the Christian mission also. Any Gentile, they insisted, could become a Christian, but first he must become a spiritual descendant of Abraham because Jesus actually came as the fulfillment of God's promise to Abraham, the father of the Hebrew people. In practice this meant that Christian converts first had to submit to the rite of circumcision and agree to observe the fundamentals of the Jewish law, thus admitting that Christianity was a modified form of Judaism!

Paul was horrified at this "revolution" in Galatia. Not only were his closest friends deserting him, but what was worse, they were in danger of losing the glorious freedom of the Christian life. If the Jewish law was still a necessity, then Christ had died in vain and Christianity had little or nothing to offer beyond what was given in Judaism! These extremists from Jerusalem were undoubtedly sincere in their concern for the welfare of the Galatian Christians, but this did not lessen Paul's bitterness or the vehemence of his reply.

His letter is from beginning to end an angry letter. He opens without his usual lengthy salutation and plunges into the heat of the controversy by showing his obvious bitterness and disappointment. His words pour out in a veritable torrent of defense and accusation as he defends his ministry and his message while accusing his opponents of ignorance and evil. He uses every means at his disposal in trying to convince the Galatians of their tragic error in following after these false teachers. Ordinarily satisfied to add his signature to letters dictated to a secretary, Paul here adds a strong statement in large letters, indicative of his deep emotion and concern.

His specific *purpose* in writing is (*a*) to defend his personal authority as an apostle, and (*b*) to defend his gospel, emphasizing the validity of Christian freedom.

The first two chapters of Galatians have been called "Paul's autobiography" because in defending himself he reveals a great deal about his part in the early life of the church. His commission as an apostle is valid, he insists, because it came, not from the Twelve, but from Christ himself! "Paul an apostle — not from men nor through man, but through Jesus Christ and God the Father, who raised him from the dead —" He calls down curses upon those who have attacked him, describing the call that came to him from Christ. After his call, he points out, he had very little to do with the other apostles, counting himself as their equal. In a council at Jerusalem the leading apostles, after reviewing his life and work, had sent him out with their full blessing. Later, Paul had even rebuked Peter with devastating effect: "I opposed him to his face, because he stood condemned." Thus he defends himself by establishing his authority as second to none among the apostles and leaders of the church.

From the point of view of the historian, an unusually high value is placed on this autobiographical sketch which Paul threw off in the heat of battle. When the relatively late date of the Gospels and the book of The Acts was established, many doubts were expressed about our ability to reconstruct with any accuracy the essentials of early Christian history. But in these chapters in Galatians, Paul takes us very close to the actual events out of which the first- and second-century church developed. These two chapters thus constitute "the bedrock of early Christian history."

In defending his gospel, or teaching, Paul's theme is salvation by faith and not by works of the law. "We ourselves, who are Jews by birth and not Gentile sinners, yet who know that a man is not justified by works of the law but through faith in Jesus Christ, even we have believed in Christ Jesus, in order to be justified by faith in Christ, and not by works of the law, because by works of the law shall no one be justified." (Gal. 2:15-16.) Paul had discovered that no matter how hard he tries, man cannot achieve salvation by obedience to the law. On the contrary, he is saved by faith in the forgiving love (grace) of God as revealed in Christ. What this means is that man, estranged, frustrated, and despairing because of his own failure, turns to God in repentance and trust only to find himself recon-

ciled and "made new." This is the basic experience that
came to the early Christians, including Paul, as such a holy
and joyful surprise. Paul's argument here is so valuable
because reconciliation is still the basic experience of the
Christian religion, though few people understand it as
such.

The apostle then strengthens his defense by showing
that salvation by faith has been a part of God's plan from
the very beginning, for Abraham was saved by faith long
before the law was revealed to men. And what had the
law achieved? Through the long centuries the law had only
succeeded in condemning men, for no one had been able
to observe it. True, it had served a temporary purpose as
our "custodian" until Christ came, like the attendant in
Greek society who took the boys through the streets to
school where he turned them over to their teacher. But
now that we are in the presence of the Teacher himself,
we no longer need the attendant. The Jewish law, mean-
ingless and misleading, can now be discarded.

In the last two chapters, Paul defends this teaching on
ethical grounds. He had been charged with destroying the
grounds for moral obligation by abolishing the law. With
all controls gone, men would live and do as they pleased.
But Paul insists that salvation by faith in Christ brings a
new kind of inner control that is far more effective than
any external law. In place of the old external control,
Christ gives men his Spirit working from within, a Spirit
that produces love, joy, peace, patience, kindness, good-
ness, faithfulness, gentleness, and self-control. The whole
basis of the ethical life is thus shifted from obedience to
an external law to the working out of a new inward motiva-
tion of purity and love through the Spirit made real by
Christ.

It would be impossible to overemphasize the significance

of this letter for Christian faith. Here in bold and blazing form is the earliest description of the basic Christian experience, salvation by faith, and the earliest description of the Christian ethical life that is rooted and grounded in love. Man cannot achieve his own salvation by obedience to works of the law. He is saved through faith in the grace of God through Christ. Nor does he live a good life by obedience to an external law, but only by the working out of love in all his relationships. From the vantage point of history we may look back and rejoice that Paul's gospel was so seriously threatened because, in the white heat of his defense, he gives a clear and powerful description of the Christian faith at its deepest levels. His words are still a ringing challenge to those in every age, including our own, who try to achieve salvation by doing good deeds. "O foolish Galatians! Who has bewitched you? . . . For freedom Christ has set us free; stand fast therefore, and do not submit again to a yoke of slavery."

2. *Problems*

Unfortunately, many serious problems arise in any attempt to comprehend the context and contents of this important letter. We are not sure where Paul wrote it, though the majority of scholars agree that he must have been in Ephesus. If so, this sets the date around A.D. 54, as we have seen, but there is no certainty about this date. We have also noted the dispute about the location of the Galatian churches, many insisting that they were located in the northern area of Galatia. This seems unlikely, however, since Paul would have to go far out of his way to visit the sparsely populated area in the north of the province. It is far more likely that the churches addressed in this letter were on the southern coast, which would be the shortest and fastest route to the west. Fortunately, these highly debated problems which continue to plague us do not detract from the religious value of the epistle.

The "large letters" at the end of the letter have also attracted a good deal of attention. "See with what large letters I am writing to you with my own hand." (Gal. 6:11.) Some have suggested that Paul had weak eyes and had to write large to see what he was writing; others insist that he was not skilled in writing and had to print out his message carefully, like a child. It is scarcely necessary to concoct such theories, however, when we feel the mood of the hour. Paul has poured out his soul and now adds a personal note in large letters for further emphasis. "Read this letter," he seems to be saying. "Read it and listen to it! Stand fast and do not submit again to a yoke of slavery!"

3. Outline

1. Paul's defense of his ministry (chs. 1 and 2)
   a. His commission from God (ch. 1:1–17)
   b. His relationship to the apostles (chs. 1:18 to 2:21)
2. Paul's defense of his gospel (chs. 3 to 6)
   a. Salvation by faith and not by law (chs. 3 and 4)
      (1) The means of salvation (ch. 3:1–14)
      (2) The place of the law (chs. 3:15 to 4:31)
   b. The ethical life of love (chs. 5 and 6)
      (1) Christian freedom (ch. 5:1–15)
      (2) Ethics of the Spirit (chs. 5:16 to 6:18)

Chapter 5

First Corinthians

1. Background

FIRST CORINTHIANS takes us closer to the daily life of the early church than any other document in our possession. It has been humorously called the most typical "church letter" in history because it opens with a fight over the preacher and closes with a collection. The chapters in between these two common situations run the gamut of concrete problems that arose in the early Christian church as the Christians tried to adjust to life in a large pagan city. What about the place of women in the church? Can Christians marry pagans? Is it permissible for a Christian to eat meat offered to idols? How can we solve party strife within the church? These and numerous similar problems which had arisen were brought to Paul's attention. In following his approach to each situation, we find ourselves embroiled in first-century arguments, yet we have the feeling that we are never far from the heart of religious experience. The ability to relate daily problems to ultimate questions of human existence was a part of Paul's greatness as a teacher.

Corinth had long been one of the most important cities of the ancient world. Located on a narrow isthmus that connects the northern and southern halves of Greece, it was a natural center for ancient Mediterranean commerce. The classic city had been destroyed by the Romans, but Julius Caesar had built a new city on the site, which soon became a vigorous and thriving center of paganism. In Paul's time it had a reputation all over the world as a city of pleasure, a fact that may account for the large number of problems raised by the Christians who lived there.

Paul first visited Corinth "with fear and much trembling" after founding churches in Philippi and Thessalonica. His mission was so successful that he remained for nearly two years, converting many pagans and establishing a vigorous Christian community that ultimately gave him more trouble than any of his other churches. The converts came from a wide variety of backgrounds; hence it was difficult to hold them together even with their common experience of Christ. They had, moreover, the typical Greek tendency toward strife and disunion. The ancient Greek spirit tended toward individualism and this, more than anything else, brought the nation to ruin. This tendency carried over into church life, so that even while Paul was living among them he had great difficulty in holding them together. When he left, the church broke up into parties and factions, and we see from his letters how hard he labored to bring the fragments into some kind of unity in Christ. He also had to face the problems raised by the great emphasis that the Greek Christians placed upon knowledge, often ignoring the moral implications of the new knowledge that Christ had brought. They were far more eager to debate than to obey. Paul's great aim in this letter is to help them see the necessity of "doing the truth" as well as knowing the truth.

Because of the great trouble this church caused Paul, he wrote the fullest and longest letters to it. He probably wrote to the Corinthians many times, for we have evidence of at least four letters within the two documents that we label Corinthians in our New Testament. In First Corinthians he mentions an earlier letter that had been misunderstood (I Cor. 5:9). Some scholars believe that we have a fragment of that letter in Second Corinthians (II Cor. 6:14 to 7:1). Then he wrote our present First Corinthians during the latter part of his long stay in Ephesus. Circumstances in the church did not improve, however, so Paul was forced to write an "angry" letter, which gave him great pain to send (II Cor. 2:4;7:8). Many interpreters are convinced that a fragment of this painful letter has been preserved in the last four chapters of our present Second Corinthians. After sending the angry letter, Paul set out for Corinth in person, but on the way received a favorable report from Titus. The apostle therefore sent a letter of reconciliation, our present Second Corinthians, chs. 1 to 9, assuring the Corinthians of his love and expressing the hope that the divisions and anger would be forgotten. The great difficulty this church caused Paul during his lifetime resulted in a rich deposit for future generations in the correspondence that became necessary in the ever-changing situation.

If First Corinthians was written from Ephesus during the latter part of Paul's stay in that city, the date is probably A.D. 55–56. His *purpose* in writing is to answer questions ("Now concerning the matters about which you wrote") and correct errors and evils that had been reported to him ("It has been reported to me by Chloe's people"). His ideas follow one another without much design or organization but most of them fall into two main categories: (*a*) theological and (*b*) ethical.

Although this letter is primarily concerned with the ethical life of the early Christians, Paul makes every question, ultimately, a religious one. He assumes or reflects theological issues on nearly every page, referring in numerous passages, for example, to the salvation that God has made available through Jesus Christ. Since this gospel of reconciliation had been the basis of his preaching in Corinth, he does not dwell on it in writing, but it is constantly present as a basic presupposition. In the first chapter he points out how saving faith in the redemptive act of God in Christ is infinitely superior to the wisdom and knowledge of men. Later, in the midst of his discussion of the resurrection, he cries out, "By the grace of God I am what I am, and his grace toward me was not in vain."

Besides numerous references to the basic experience of reconciliation, Paul addresses himself to one specific theological problem in the longest and fullest chapter in all of his writings (I Cor., ch. 15). The problem of immortality had been raised by the report that some members of the Corinthian church did not believe in resurrection. As Greeks they probably believed in some kind of immortality of the soul, but not in a bodily resurrection after death. Immortality of the soul was a typical Greek concept, appearing often in their philosophy, poetry, and drama, but Paul, reflecting his Jewish training, could not conceive of continued life apart from a body. Unlike his fellow Jews, however, he did not believe in the resurrection of the physical body that was of the earth and would perish. He was certain, on the contrary, that the Holy God who gives every form of life an appropriate body may be trusted to clothe us in a "spiritual body" when we die. Elsewhere he speaks of this as a "glorious" body (Phil. 3:21) and maintains that Christ had risen from the dead in just such a new or spiritual body. Paul's great concern here is to maintain personal or individual identity after death, in opposition to the Greek concept of immortality in which man's spirit loses its individuality. Paul insists on the necessity of resurrection in a spiritual body, which means that we survive as personal beings with individuality and self-identity. In this way, the life-transforming relationship with God through Christ that we have known on earth continues in the life to come.

In developing his argument here, Paul reports the resurrection of Jesus in a passage of supreme historical value (I Cor. 15:3–8). It comes from a period about twenty-five years after the event and long before the Gospel accounts were written down. Paul tells us that what he is writing is in full agreement with the reports of the disciples who first experienced the presence of the risen Lord. This passage is thus the primary historical document for the resurrection of Jesus.

In addition to these theological matters, First Corinthians contains our most detailed account of the ethical problems of early Christianity. Those who had been reconciled to God through Christ found themselves living a new kind of life, so new, in fact, they needed constant instruction. They were transformed into "new beings," eagerly seeking to live a new life of love, but the love was different from anything they had known before. It is impossible to convey in English the meaning of this concept of love, since we have only one word where the Greeks had three. In speaking of the new life of love that grows out of reconciliation with God, Jesus and Paul do not use the word for physical love nor the word for friendship. They speak of *agapē*, a universal, selfless, redemptive, compassionate concern for others. This kind of love is the basic principle of the Christian ethical life. Christian ethics is simply the working out of this kind of love in every relationship and experience of life. In First Corinthians we have a superb description of the basic principle and many examples of its application to specific situations.

The principle of *agapē* is the theme of the thirteenth chapter, often called Paul's "hymn to love." It is without doubt the most magnificent passage in the Pauline writings, and belongs with the more important passages in the literature of the world. The love (*agapē*) that is the heart and center of the new life of the Christian believer is pictured in all its fullness and power. No words adequately describe the power of this "hymn" which should be set in poetic form for fullest effect. Paul writes and "sings" here of a love that is even greater than faith or hope!

In a sense, all of First Corinthians centers around this thirteenth chapter. One by one, Paul takes up the problems faced by the early Christians and shows how all of them can be resolved through the power of love now made available in their relationship to Christ.

First, he discusses the party divisions that had arisen because of a quarrel over the effectiveness of preachers (I Cor., chs. 1 to 4). Many had been struck by the eloquence of Apollos, others by the authority of Peter. But Paul insists that all Christians are bound together in a love that transcends party strife and argumentation. Each teacher and preacher has a contribution to make, all working together as "fellow workmen for God."

A case of gross immorality (I Cor., ch. 5) is next discussed, followed by the problem of Christians going to pagan law courts in order to solve their grievances against one another (I Cor., ch. 6). The new life of love, Paul insists, is a life of moral purity, and those who persist in immorality thereby separate themselves from God and from the fellowship of believers. He also insists that the power of love should be so strong within the fellowship that all differences should be settled there rather than before the eyes of the world.

The discussion of marriage that follows (I Cor., ch. 7) has caused a great deal of misunderstanding due to its apparent ascetic attitude toward marriage and divorce. "It is well for a man not to touch a woman." In evaluating Paul's teaching on this matter we must remember that he expected the immediate return of Jesus. Since the time was so short, the unmarried should remain unmarried, and the married should not separate. The important thing was that persons should not let themselves be distracted from their preparations for the coming of the Lord. Marriage is not a sin, but it is apt to be distracting!

Concerning meat offered to idols (I Cor., chs. 8 to 10), Paul's words are more relevant for our time than we might imagine. He addresses himself to the first-century problem faced by Christians who found that most of the available meat in the markets had been sacrificed before a pagan idol. Some of the Christians were fearful lest they sin by eating such "consecrated" meat, but Paul reassures them. Their new-found relationship to God through Christ had raised them above such considerations, so there was no harm so far as their own consciences were concerned. The real problem was that some of the weaker brethren might be misled and harmed by seeing Christians eat such meat. Hence, Paul's famous dictum: "Therefore, if food is a cause of my brother's falling, I will never eat meat, lest I cause my brother to fall" (I Cor. 8:13). Only those who know the power of *agapē* can understand and apply such a counsel of selfless concern.

Paul's words concerning the veiling of women (I Cor. 11:1–16) reflect his Oriental background and seem irrelevant today, but many persons in our time have expressed a longing for greater modesty in women and greater respect for women on the part of men. We must agree, however, that social customs change, and we should not make the mistake of insisting on slavish obedience to ethical ideas in the New Testament that do not apply to our own vastly different cultural situation.

After a brief reprimand for the lack of love and reverence that the Corinthians were showing in the observance of the Lord's Supper (I Cor. 11:17–34), Paul enters into a lengthy discussion of spiritual gifts (I Cor., chs. 12 to 14). Primitive Christian worship was often accompanied by outbursts of enthusiasm that included strange cries, trances, visions, and ecstatic dancing. After examining these practices, Paul concludes that they are far inferior to expressions of love. All "gifts" are worthless apart from love, which is the "more excellent way."

In this manner Paul applies the basic principle of love to the complexities of daily life in the church at Corinth. In doing so, he performed an incalculable service to Christian faith, for Jesus had taught and lived among the simple villages of Galilee, leading many to label his ethic of love as impractical and irrelevant in more complex societies. But Paul shows us the relevance of *agapē* in the thriving pagan city of Corinth and thus demonstrates its universal significance. It is for every city, for every Christian, in every situation of life. Paul's first letter to Corinth is a monument to the universality and timelessness of Christian love.

2. Problems

The chief problem surrounding the Corinthian letters is that of chronology and arrangement. We have suggested that there were four letters and perhaps many more. In view of this fact, it should not surprise us to find New Testament scholars debating about the order in which the letters were written and the occasion that gave rise to them. We have already suggested a simple outline that clears up much of the confusion, but all conclusions on such matters must be regarded as tentative at best.

Because of the length of First Corinthians and its apparent lack of unity, some have suggested that it is a compilation of letters and fragments. There is no real reason for breaking it up, however, particularly in view of the unity of a sort that we find in its central principle of love. The principle is applied to many disconnected problems, but this is probably due to the order in which the problems were presented to Paul by letter and report from Corinth. Diverse on the surface, the material in First Corinthians is held together by love.

3. Outline

1. Party strife and disunity (chs. 1 to 4)
2. A case of gross immorality (ch. 5)
3. Christian lawsuits in pagan courts (ch. 6)
4. Marriage and divorce (ch. 7)
5. Meat offered to idols (chs. 8 to 10)
6. The veiling of women (ch. 11:1–16)
7. The observance of the Lord's Supper (ch. 11:17–34)
8. Love as the supreme gift (chs. 12 to 14)
9. Immortality and resurrection (ch. 15)
10. Concerning the collection (ch. 16)

Chapter 6

Second Corinthians

1. Background

FIRST CORINTHIANS was a failure. This seems incredible to us in view of the significant role that it has played in the history of the church, but it obviously failed to achieve Paul's original intention. Disunity in the church and disloyalty to Paul increased to such a degree that the apostle had to make a hurried visit to Corinth. But the visit, like the letter, was unsuccessful. Upon his return to Ephesus, Paul therefore wrote an "angry letter," so bitter that he later wished he had not sent it. Then he crossed over into Macedonia, anxious about the result of his severe attitude, where he was met by Titus, who came with good news. The Corinthians had taken the message to heart and renewed their loyalty to Paul. Filled with gratitude, he wrote a "letter of reconciliation," sending it on ahead with Titus and following it with a personal visit shortly there-after. In our present Second Corinthians we have all or part of both the angry letter and the letter of reconcilia-tion.

The angry letter, written "out of much affliction and anguish of heart and with many tears," is mentioned more than once in the first part of Second Corinthians (II Cor. 2:3–4;7:8). Most scholars and commentators, long puzzled over the abrupt change of mood that occurs at the end of ch. 9, are now convinced that the last chapters (II Cor., chs. 10 to 13) are a part of the angry letter written by Paul from Ephesus about A.D. 57. Injured and incensed at the result of the earlier letter (First Corinthians) and personal visit, Paul's *purpose* now is to express his anguish and anger at their unfaithfuless to him in following false teachers and apostles, who are leading them astray.

The main approach he takes is that of personal defense. This passage, like the early chapters of Galatians, is extremely valuable as a kind of autobiography of Paul, written in deep emotion because of the seriousness of the attacks upon his ministry and message. He defends himself against insults and criticisms and then, "foolish" as it is, begins to "boast" like his rivals. The hardships he has endured for the gospel give him much more to boast about and raise him far above the "superlative apostles" who have been leading the Corinthians astray. Following Paul through his famous "catalogue of hardships" (II Cor. 11:21–29) leaves the reader dazed and breathless. Reference is made in several places in his letters to his suffering on behalf of Christ, but nowhere else is it reviewed with such deep emotion. These few lines, so intensely personal and forceful, have seldom been matched anywhere in literature.

Equally moving is Paul's description of his spiritual conflicts. He points out how he has been gifted with "visions and revelations of the Lord," lifted up "to the third heaven," caught up "into Paradise." But in order to keep him from being too proud and elated over his spiritual accomplishments he was given a "thorn in the flesh" that caused him terrible agony. There has been a great deal of

speculation about the nature of the thorn in the flesh, since
Paul does not describe it in detail. More than likely, how-
ever, it was some form of neurotic attack that humiliated
him before enemies and friends alike. Three times he had
prayed about it, but God had answered, "My grace is suf-
ficient for you, for my power is made perfect in weakness."
For the sake of Christ, then, he will be "content with weak-
nesses, insults, hardships, persecutions, and calamities; for
when I am weak, then I am strong" (II Cor. 12:10).

Seldom do we get as close to Paul as we do in these
chapters where a mood of burning invective prevails from
beginning to end. Still, he breaks through time and again
with expressions of deep affection for the Corinthians. In
fact, his great love for them made him feel their disloyalty
all the more. We have no way of knowing how much
longer the original letter may have been than the frag-
ment we now possess in these last four chapters. But we
have enough to understand Paul's deep regret at having
to write such a letter to those whom he loved, even more
his regret in sending it. He loved them deeply, but he
could not bear their rejection of him in favor of those
whom he bitingly calls "superlative apostles." It is not dif-
ficult to picture him sending this letter and then waiting
anxiously to see what effect it would have.

Fortunately, the result was even better than expected.
This is perfectly obvious from the whole tone of the letter
of reconciliation (II Cor., chs. 1 to 9) he wrote after hear-
ing the good news from Titus. The Corinthians had done
a complete about-face, had seen the error of their dis-
loyalty to Paul, and had rejected one of the false teachers
with such indignation that Paul had to intercede on his
behalf. Paul's main *purpose* in writing is to confirm his
reconciliation with the Corinthians after learning of their
renewed faithfulness in him. He wrote while in Macedonia

en route to Corinth probably very soon after the painful letter, in A.D. 57.

The mood of this letter is a complete reversal of the anger that dominated his earlier communication to them. Now he is seeking harmony, peace, and comfort. In the opening paragraph he uses the word "comfort" ten times and then returns to it again and again. Bursting with joy and gratitude, he expresses great love and compassion for these friends whom he has now won back to his side. He reviews some of the issues that had divided them, but now in a tone of gentleness and cordiality, reminding them of the deep anguish he had suffered during the period of estrangement and misunderstanding.

As if to heal the bonds of separation, he speaks again and again of God's unspeakable gift in Jesus Christ. Remembrance of Christ lifts us above earthly divisions and entanglements and makes us into new creatures who begin life all over again! "Therefore, if any one is in Christ, he is a new creation; the old has passed away, behold, the new has come." No longer the terrible estrangement from God, no longer the unbearable guilt of our sin against God and against our fellows! We are now new creatures, living a new life with God at the center. Reconciliation with God is the basic theme of this letter, since Paul knows that only in God can men be reconciled to one another. We have been emphasizing this experience of reconciliation through Christ as the major concern of all the New Testament writers, though they express it in a wide variety of ways. But seldom, if ever, do any of them surpass the mood of radiant joy and holy surprise that Paul shares with his Corinthian friends after the storms of their differences have passed.

Closely related to this central theme is the brief discussion of eternal life. In First Corinthians he had expressed the belief that men must wait for the general resurrection before they would be clothed with the "spiritual body" and enter into the fullness of life with God in Christ. But now he holds that the new body is already prepared. The believer will enter into the next life at the moment of death, indeed is already entering into it as he slowly dies to the world. "So we do not lose heart. Though our outer nature is wasting away, our inner nature is being renewed every day. For this slight momentary affliction is preparing for us an eternal weight of glory beyond all comparison, because we look not to the things that are seen but to the things that are unseen; for the things that are seen are transient, but the things that are unseen are eternal." (II Cor. 4:16–18.) In this way, Paul rounds out his earlier teaching.

Many persons have found the abrupt ending of the epistle somewhat disappointing. After expressing deep religious insight in a mood of strong personal affection for his friends, he suddenly begins to talk about the collection! Even Paul seems to sense some discontinuity, for his practical arguments in favor of the collection are awkward and forced. Then suddenly, as if aware of the futility of such appeals, he returns to his central theme, and states the true basis for Christian giving: "Thanks be to God for his inexpressible gift!" So far as we know, this is the last word of the letter and the last word that Paul ever wrote to his friends in Corinth. It is a fitting close because it is the dominant mood of Paul's entire apostolic ministry.

Shortly after sending this letter, Paul arrived in Corinth. We are not told how he was received, but he evidently found himself once again among friends who loved him and provided him with freedom from anxiety and controversy. During the last weeks of his stay with them he wrote his letter to the Romans. Part of its tremendous power surely comes from the atmosphere of Christian love out of which he wrote, an atmosphere provided by his Corinthian friends, whom Paul calls living "letters of recommendation" from Christ to be known and read by all men.

2. Problems

As already indicated, the chief problem of Second Corinthians is its unity. Many attempts have been made to account for the abrupt change of mood between chs. 9 and 10. It has been suggested that Paul was interrupted after writing the first part of the letter. When he returned to it after a few days his mood had completely changed. Some have maintained that Paul's main purpose was reconciliation, but when he came to the end of the letter he remembered certain points of issue and burst into anger.

Such attempts to explain the apparent lack of unity in this letter are psychologically improbable, even for a man of changing moods and emotions such as Paul was. It is far more reasonable to explain the incongruity by the two very different situations that occurred at different times in Paul's relations with the church in Corinth. The spirit, style, and contents of the two sections support this view. Further evidence is found in the repetition of certain themes in the last letter, but now in a very different mood. He includes, for example, another catalogue of hardships (II Cor. 6:1–10). It is not very likely that he would have included two lists so similar in the same letter. We can also understand how the friends of Paul who collected his letters would wish to soften the sharpness of the angry letter by attaching it to the end of the serene and friendly correspondence that actually followed it in order. Religious value was more important than chronological sequence to the early Christians, a fact that has caused modern scholars no end of difficulty. For these many reasons, we look upon Second Corinthians as a combination of two major letters from the hand of Paul.

In conclusion, it should be noted that Second Corinthians also contains a small fragment of the very first letter that Paul wrote to this church. In First Corinthians he mentions an earlier letter that has caused some misunderstanding (I Cor. 5:9). He had warned the church members to stay away from immoral persons, and they had misunderstood the intention of his remarks. It seems quite likely that II Cor. 6:14 to 7:1 is a fragment of this earlier letter. It contains just such a warning against immoral company and it is completely out of place in its present context.

To summarize, therefore, we have evidence of four letters that Paul wrote to his friends in Corinth: (*a*) an early letter (II Cor. 6:14 to 7:1); (*b*) our present First Corinthians; (*c*) the angry letter (II Cor., chs. 10 to 13); and (*d*) the letter of reconciliation (II Cor., chs. 1 to 9). This wealth of material affords such keen insight into the life and thought of Paul and the early church that it holds a unique place among the priceless documents of our Christian faith.

3. Outline

"THE ANGRY LETTER"

1. Paul's personal defense (chs. 10:1 to 12:13)
   a. His sincerity (chs. 10:1 to 11:6)
   b. His self-support (ch. 11:7–15)
   c. His suffering for the gospel (chs. 11:16 to 12:13)
2. Closing appeals (chs. 12:14 to 13:14)
   a. Warning about his approaching visit (chs. 12:14 to 13:10)
   b. Salutation and benediction (ch. 13:11–14)

"THE LETTER OF RECONCILIATION"

Second Corinthians

The Letter of Reconciliation
1. Gratitude and reconciliation (chs. 1 to 7, except chs.
   6:14 to 7:1)
a. Salutation and thanksgiving (ch. 1:1–11)
b. Review of strained relations (chs. 1:12 to 2:17)
c. Vindication of his apostleship (chs. 3:1 to 6:10)
   (1) His life and suffering (chs. 3:1 to 4:6)
   (2) Eternal life in Christ (chs. 4:7 to 5:10)
   (3) Reconciliation with God through Christ (chs.
       5:11 to 6:13)
d. Appeal for complete reconciliation (ch. 7:2–16)
2. Concerning the collection (chs. 8 and 9)

Chapter 7

Romans

1. Background

THE LETTER to the Romans, one of the most awe-inspiring books in the Bible, was written when Paul reached a crucial turning point in his career. Eager to make the gospel known throughout the Mediterranean world, he concentrated first on the province in the east. The result of his labor could be measured in the vigor of the churches at Thessalonica, Philippi, Galatia, Corinth, and Ephesus — all centers from which the good news could spread because of its own intrinsic value. Now he was free to concentrate on new frontiers in the west, especially the great city of Rome.

The capital of Rome had a particular appeal to him, figuring crucially in his plan to spread the gospel throughout the Empire. There was already a flourishing church there, but not knowing Paul or his gospel, it was in danger of being led astray by false teachers, as the Galatians and Corinthians had been. Paul knew that his mission in the west would be hopeless if his enemies entrenched themselves in the capital city and spread false information about him throughout the provinces yet to be won to

Christ. Standing at this turning point in his career, Paul saw the necessity of conquering Rome for Christ and for the gospel of Christ as Paul understood it.

Before he could launch this great crusade, however, there was one vital piece of unfinished business, the collection for the poor in Jerusalem. The apostle had been working on this project for many months, confident that this example of love would help bind the Jewish and Greek Christians closer together. The plan called for one or two delegates from each church to meet in Corinth and travel together to Jerusalem with Paul. Thus, before he could move east toward Rome, the city of Christianity's future, he had to sail once more to Jerusalem, the city of her past.

While waiting in Corinth with leisure on his hands, he wrote the letter to the Romans. Usually dated A.D. 57–58, it is without doubt the most ambitious of all his writings. In form it is a letter, in content a formal theological treatise. Since Paul did not know the Roman Christians personally, he could not use the intimate spontaneous style of his other epistles. He is much more formal in his approach, giving evidence of studied concern for literary form and systematic presentation, but this does not mean that Romans is any less of a letter than his other correspondence. The occasion simply called for a different approach, and Paul, eager to be all things to all men for Christ, easily adapts himself to the new situation.

The great apostle was obviously convinced that he would soon be visiting the Roman Christians in person. His *purpose* in writing is to introduce himself and his message by presenting the main features of his thought in a systematic argument that emphasizes (*a*) justification by faith as the heart of the gospel and (*b*) the universality of the gospel.

His dominant theme throughout is the experience of

justification by faith made possible by God's mighty act in Jesus Christ. His whole work is like a stately symphony in which the composer reveals his theme at the beginning and then explores it in every possible way. The mood changes, the pace varies, the theme is unchanging. At the end of each movement of thought, Paul restates the theme in words of surging power and beauty, only to move on to some new phase of his subject. Those who allow themselves to be caught up in this letter can easily understand why it has had such an incredible influence on countless Christians including Augustine, Luther, Calvin, and Wesley. It explores and describes the basic experience of the Christian religion with unmatched power and effectiveness.

The first five chapters constitute a coherent unit in themselves. After opening greetings, Paul states the theme that will dominate the letter: "For I am not ashamed of the gospel: it is the power of God for salvation to every one who has faith, to the Jew first and also to the Greek. For in it the righteousness of God is revealed through faith for faith; as it is written, 'He who through faith is righteous shall live'" (Rom. 1:16–17). This is a quotation from Habakkuk, the Old Testament prophet, who meant that a righteous man will survive by his steadfastness. But Paul takes it in a glorious new sense, meaning that those who become righteous by faith in Christ will obtain (eternal) life.

In the remainder of the first chapter he shows how the Gentiles have become estranged from God, even though his eternal power and deity were available to them through creation. The Jews (Rom., ch. 2) are also estranged from God, though they have even less of an excuse, since God was revealed to them through the law. All have sinned and fallen short of the glory of God, but "they are justified by his grace as a gift, through the redemption which is in Christ Jesus, whom God put forward as an expiation by his blood, to be received by faith" (Rom. 3:24–25). Neither by wisdom nor by works of the law can we become upright and accepted by God, but only by an act of faith in which we repent and accept the grace of God.

Having reached a climax in ch. 3, Paul now shows how the histories of Abraham (Rom., ch. 4) and Adam (Rom., ch. 5) support his position. As in Galatia and Corinth, there would be teachers in Rome insisting that Christ was the fulfillment of God's agreement with Abraham, thus the necessity of becoming a Jew before becoming a Christian. In opposition, Paul insists that Abraham won God's approval through faith and not through the law. Thus the experience of Abraham becomes evidence in support of the way of faith. Adam, on the other hand, has infected the whole race with his sin, but now a man has come who erases completely the results of that sin. "If, because of one man's trespass, death reigned through that one man, much more will those who receive the abundance of grace and the free gift of righteousness reign in life through the one man Jesus Christ." (Rom. 5:17.) In this way Paul completes the first movement of his thought.

The second movement (Rom., chs. 6 to 8) explores the consequences of the life of faith. Chapter 6 shows the man of faith saved from sin; ch. 7, the man of faith saved from the law; and ch. 8, the man of faith exalted in his new relationship with God. Nowhere in Christian thought do we find a deeper awareness of the despair and futility of sin and of trying to save ourselves through works of the law. It is no accident that the recent theological reaction against modern man's easygoing attitude toward sin is rooted in Paul's letter to the Romans. The apostle speaks to our condition when he ends his exploration of sin and

law with the cry of despair: "Wretched man that I am!
Who will deliver me from this body of death?"

His answer (Rom., ch. 8) brings us to another climactic
expression of his theme as he describes the exalted life of
a man whose justification by faith enables him to enter
into a new kind of life with God. The whole creation has
been groaning in travail until now, waiting for redemption.
But now the redemption has come, and we know that
nothing shall separate us from the love of Christ, not tribu-
lation, or distress, or persecution, or famine, or nakedness,
or peril, or sword! "No, in all these things we are more than
conquerors through him who loved us. For I am sure that
neither death, nor life, nor angels, nor principalities, nor
things present, nor things to come, nor powers, nor height,
nor depth, nor anything else in all creation, will be able
to separate us from love of God in Christ Jesus our Lord."
(Rom. 8:37–39.) This eighth chapter of Romans is uni-
versally acclaimed as one of the most dazzling and per-
suasive expressions of Christian faith in all of Christian
literature.

In one sense Paul has exhausted himself and his reader
by this point, but he feels the necessity of adding a double
appendix. The first part (Rom., chs. 9 to 11) attempts to
explain the failure of the Jews to accept Jesus Christ who
was the fulfillment of their own religion, the Messiah fore-
told by their own prophets. This Jewish rejection of Chris-
tianity must have been a difficult thing for the Gentiles to
understand. Paul tries to give an explanation, pointing out
that the disobedience of Israel was part of God's purpose,
making it possible for the gospel to be carried to the Gen-
tiles. The redemption of the Gentiles will in turn bring the
Jews into the new relationship with God so that ultimately
all will be saved. God has not abandoned his people but
is working for their salvation in a new and more powerful

way. "O the depth of the riches and wisdom and knowl-
edge of God! How unsearchable are his judgments and
how inscrutable his ways ! . . . For from him and through
him and to him are all things. To him be glory forever.
Amen." (Rom. 11:33, 36.)

In these same chapters, Paul sets forth a doctrine of pre-
destination that has caused untold difficulty in later the-
ology. His intention is to stress God's initiation of man's
salvation: man is never redeemed by any action on his own
part, but always by acceptance of God's initial act in Jesus
Christ. Thus salvation is available to all. But Paul's particu-
lar emphasis on this fact led later Christians to believe that
from the beginning of time some men are elected to salva-
tion and others condemned to eternal punishment. In spite
of the widespread acceptance of this idea through the in-
fluence of Augustine and Calvin, there is no evidence that
Paul intended any such interpretation of his thought.

The second part of the appendix to this letter (Rom.,
chs. 12 to 15) is of major significance because of its de-
scription of the moral life of those who have been saved
by faith. Paul knew that the experience of justification by
faith inevitably leads to a new life of love. This new life
is the fruit of man's new relationship to God. It is note-
worthy that Galatians and Romans, the two letters that
best express Paul's doctrine of justification, both end with
detailed instruction on the daily conduct of the Christian
life. Chapter 12 in Romans has been compared with the
Sermon on the Mount in its effectiveness in describing the
Christian life of love, but unfortunately it has been over-
shadowed by the powerful message in the rest of the let-
ter. Chapter 13 is a discussion of the Christian's relation
to the state, a matter of great importance to church mem-
bers living in the capital of the Empire. Paul insists on the
necessity of good citizenship, both as a matter of prudence

and of Christian conscience. The final two chapters (Rom., chs. 14 to 15) complete the argument and end with an outline of plans for the future. In his closing words, Paul asks the Roman Christians to pray for him, "so that by God's will I may come to you with joy and be refreshed in your company. The God of peace be with you all. Amen" (Rom. 15:32–33).

Throughout all the discussion of justification by faith there is a secondary theme on the universality of the gospel. In most places Christianity began as a movement within Judaism, a fact that pagans must have found very confusing. Equally confusing was the fact that Paul had sharply cut his ties with the law and with the Jewish past. Some may have regarded him with suspicion because of this break with his own tradition. It is therefore imperative for the Romans to understand that the message of Christ is a universal message intended for all mankind. The gospel is the power of God unto salvation for all men. Christianity is a new and higher religion offered to mankind by God through Jesus Christ, the Savior of "the world."

Because of the universal spirit of Romans, it is often described as a missionary letter. In content it appears to be a theological treatise, but Paul's ultimate intention may have been quite practical. He was moving out into a new field, entering the life of a church that was of vital importance in his plans for evangelizing the Empire. He is extremely anxious for these Christians to understand, even before he comes to them, that the gospel he preaches is for all mankind. It is not at all surprising, in view of this concern, that Paul's words in Romans have been quoted throughout the history of the missionary movement in support of the evangelical interests of the church. Paul's gospel is the power of God for salvation to *every one* who has faith!

2. Problems

The discerning reader will have noticed the omission of ch. 16 from the discussion of the contents of the epistle. This closing chapter is the source of much debate among interpreters. It consists of an introduction of "our sister Phoebe" and a long series of greetings that mention no less than twenty-four persons by name. More than a century ago scholars began to wonder how Paul would know so many persons in Rome. It was also noted that many of those mentioned were associated with Paul's work in Ephesus and that most had Greek rather than Roman names. For these and other reasons it is now generally believed that this last chapter is a separate note intended for the church in Ephesus. Paul's *purpose* in the note is to introduce Phoebe, a deaconess, to his friends there, and he takes advantage of this opportunity to greet many of them in a personal way. A note sent to friends with whom he had lived for more than two years would exhibit just the familiarity and informality that we find here.

Another serious problem in Romans is raised by the presence of four benedictions (Rom. 15:13; 15:33; 16:24; 16:27). The first probably indicates the close of Paul's main argument in Romans, the second, the close of the letter itself. The third is the close of the note to Ephesus, while the fourth is a formal doxology, added by a later hand.

3. Outline

1. Justification by faith as the way of salvation (chs. 1 to 5)
   a. The Gentiles estranged from God (ch. 1)
   b. The Jews estranged from God (ch. 2)
   c. Justification by faith as the way to God (ch. 3)

   d. Proof from the history of Abraham (ch. 4)
   e. Proof from the history of Adam (ch. 5)
2. Consequences of justification by faith (chs. 6 to 8)
   a. The man of faith as saved from sin (ch. 6)
   b. The man of faith as saved from the law (ch. 7)
   c. Exaltation of the man of faith (ch. 8)
3. Appendix: the failure of the Jews (chs. 9 to 11)
4. Appendix: the moral life of the man of faith (chs. 12 to 15)

Chapter 8

Colossians

1. Background

WHEN PAUL wrote his letter to the Roman Christians expressing a desire to visit them he didn't know that he would arrive as a prisoner about to die! The swift chain of events that so radically altered the course of his life began in Jerusalem where he had taken the collection for the poor. There he was mobbed and arrested on a charge of instigating a riot in the Temple. After imprisonment in Caesarea for two years, he appealed to Caesar and was taken to Rome to stand trial before the emperor, who held him in prison for three more years. The book of The Acts unfortunately ends with Paul still in prison, but other evidence leads us to believe that he was tried and executed by Nero Caesar. He had longed to visit his Roman friends, little knowing that he would spend his last days among them.

During the years of the Roman imprisonment, he wrote the so-called "Epistles of the Captivity," or prison letters. His Philippian friends upon hearing of his needs sent him funds that made it possible for him to live in relative comfort, and though he was still under arrest, the circumstances enabled him to write letters to his friends. A man of amazing energy, he undoubtedly welcomed the opportunity to use his enforced leisure in this useful and creative way.

Two of these prison letters went to Colossae, one to the church in that city and another to an individual named Philemon, whose slave had run away. The Colossian church had been established several years before while Paul was working in Ephesus. His assistants had moved out into Asia and one of them, Epaphras, had carried on a successful mission in the Lycus valley. Colossae, about a hundred miles east of Ephesus, had thus become a center of Christian influence as an indirect result of Paul's labor. Though he never visited the region, he felt responsible for the Christians there. We can understand his concern when Epaphras visited him in Rome with a report of trouble in the church.

The disorder was caused by self-styled teachers in the church who denied the supremacy of Christ and insisted that many "truths" from pagan religion were necessary to complete the gospel. Specifically, the Colossian Christians were being taught that there were many intermediate "beings" between God and man, a kind of "chain of command" that had to be followed by those who approached God. Christ was the greatest of these beings, but he was only one among many. Through reflection, self-discipline, and asceticism (fasts, vigils, and secret rites) men could rise above the material world into this realm of spiritual beings.

This Colossian heresy was the precursor of a powerful movement known as Gnosticism that later in the century threatened the very existence of the church. We meet it often in the Johannine letters and in other later New Testament writings. For Paul, however, it presented a new kind of problem. He had experienced great opposition from Jewish Christians who were trying to make Christianity a branch of Judaism. Now the trouble came from the other side, from pagan Christians who were merging pagan philosophy with the new religion. In doing so, they were denying supremacy to Christ, and creating a class system within the church. Those who possessed the secret or esoteric knowledge about the spirit world were claiming superiority over other Christians. In view of these unfortunate developments we can understand why Paul instantly moved to stamp out the heretical movement that was so dangerously perverting basic Christian ideas.

The apostle wrote from Rome about A.D. 60–61, just as soon as Epaphras reported the trouble to him. His specific *purpose* in writing is to defend his gospel against the Colossian heresy by emphasizing (*a*) the supremacy of Jesus Christ and (*b*) the absolute adequacy of justification by faith.

Paul's own overwhelming experience of Christ left him with no patience for those who were elevating and worshiping other cosmic beings. Christ alone is the Redeemer. Any attempt to approach God through other powers, forces, or beings is both false and misleading. Since Christ is the head of creation, the worship of him makes all other worship unnecessary. He is also the head of the church in whom "all the fullness of God was pleased to dwell." The tattered fragments and patches from the old religions should be totally discarded, not sewed onto the new and seamless garment of the gospel. In this way Paul seeks to stress the uniqueness of Christ with such compelling force that the Colossians will see the utter futility of worshiping "angels" and cosmic beings.

Having established the supremacy of Christ, Paul next shows how men enter the presence of God, not through esoteric knowledge and secret rites, but through faith in Christ. "And you, who once were estranged and hostile in mind, doing evil deeds, he has now reconciled in his body of flesh by his death . . . provided that you continue in the faith, stable and steadfast, not shifting from the hope of the gospel which you heard." (Col. 1:21–23.) Those who were estranged from God have been reconciled to him. Those who were "dead" have been made alive. Those who were crushed under the weight of sin have been released. Those whose lives were empty have come to fullness of life in him, "for in him the whole fulness of deity dwells bodily."

Much of the language in this letter is difficult to understand because it reflects the jargon of the heretics in Colossae. But the main form of the argument is very clear. In opposition to the angelic beings of the heretics, Paul proclaims the uniqueness of Jesus Christ. In contrast to their emphasis on special knowledge and secret worship, he exalts the experience of justification by faith.

Because of the nature of the problem he was facing, the apostle speaks more directly about the nature of Christ in this letter than in any other place in his writings. For this reason it is often called Paul's "Christological letter." Among other things it presents for the first time a doctrine concerning Christ that was to play a major role in later Christian thought. Philo of Alexandria, the noted Jewish teacher, had spoken about the "Word" or "Logos," a creative principle within the being of God. This principle goes forth from God, according to Philo, in the work of creation and revelation. Paul, here in Colossians, introduces the idea that Christ is this divine creative principle, an idea that assumes much larger proportions in Hebrews and becomes one of the themes of the Fourth Gospel.

Paul, as usual, moves from theology to ethics in the

closing lines of his message. Even when combating heresy he expressed great concern for the daily conduct of the Christian life. In this case he discusses problems of personal conduct and the relationships that should exist among members of a Christian family. Finally, he considers in detail the relations between masters and their slaves. It is easy to see why this problem was uppermost in his mind, for he was about to write a personal letter to a member of the church in Colossae on behalf of a runaway slave.

2. *Problems*

We have assumed throughout our discussion that Paul's prison epistles were written from Rome. There are some, however, who believe they were written during some period of imprisonment in Ephesus. Evidence for such a view arises in a variety of places: (*a*) The companions whom Paul mentions in the letter were with him earlier in Ephesus. (*b*) Onesimus, the runaway slave, could hardly have made it as far as Rome. (*c*) Paul seems to be in frequent contact with his churches in Asia, but this would have been impossible from the great distance of Rome under ancient travel conditions.

These arguments are not convincing. We do not know of any imprisonment in Ephesus, though we do know that he went through more than one crisis there. Even if we grant that such a crisis led to imprisonment, however, the circumstances were not the kind that would give him leisure for writing letters. Rome, moreover, was the center of the "world," in frequent communication with the rest of the Empire. It is not at all surprising to find a runaway slave using it as a refuge and Paul's friends gathering there in a time of crisis. All available evidence tends to support the traditional view that the last letters of Paul were writ-

ten from prison in Rome where he was about to be
martyred.

3. *Outline*

1. Greetings (ch. 1:1–14)
2. The supremacy of Jesus Christ (chs. 1:15 to 2:7)
3. The adequacy of justification by faith (ch. 2:8–23)
4. Ethical teaching (chs. 3:1 to 4:6)
5. Farewell (ch. 4:7–18)

Chapter 9

Philemon

1. Background

SLAVERY WAS one of the greatest evils in the ancient world. The economic system depended upon slave labor and the military conquests of the Roman armies provided vast numbers of conquered people for the slave markets of the large cities. Under such a system, where there was a constant fear of slave rebellions and uprisings, runaway slaves were treated with terrible cruelty. They were often tortured, compelled to fight wild animals in the arena, or unmercifully beaten as an example to other slaves who might be harboring dreams of freedom. Paul was therefore taking a great risk when he sent a runaway slave back to his master with an accompanying letter. We can well understand why he used all his powers of persuasion in the letter we now possess as one of our briefest New Testament documents.

It is not surprising that Onesimus had made his way to Rome after running away from Philemon, his master. Where better to change his identity and lose himself than in the teeming streets of the great cosmopolitan center? Somehow he came to know Paul, who introduced him to the Christian life and looked upon him as a son: "I am sending him back to you, sending my very heart." Knowing the dangers Onesimus faced, Paul sent a personal note to Philemon, his master, appealing to him as a brother in Christ to be merciful.

The letter was composed in Rome at the same time as the letter to the Colossian church, A.D. 60–61, and was sent with Onesimus and Tychicus, a messenger. Paul's *purpose* is to protect Onesimus from punishment and win forgiveness for him from his Christian master.

The letter has been called one of the most charming ever written. It is written with great warmth and persuasiveness, yet with a note of authority that cannot be ignored. Paul even hints that he would like to have Onesimus returned to him, but he does not press this request too far. He also includes other Christians in the letter, thus bringing social pressure to bear on Philemon, the kind of social pressure that arose because the bonds of love were so strong in the early Christian community.

We have no way of knowing whether Paul's letter was successful. It is interesting to note, however, that fifty years after Paul wrote the letter, one of the early church leaders, Ignatius of Antioch, sent a letter to the church in Ephesus in which he speaks a great deal about their bishop — Onesimus. He emphasizes the name and seems to know about the letter to Philemon. We cannot be sure that this is the same Onesimus, but it is worth speculating on the possibility that the runaway slave, Paul's "son," became the leader of one of the strongest churches in the first century.

2. Problems

The chief problem relating to this letter is not historical but ethical. Neither here, nor elsewhere, does Paul raise any protest against the terrible institution of slavery, the source of untold cruelty and suffering. Many persons, charmed by his letter to Philemon, are nevertheless deeply troubled by his failure to see the wider implications of sending a slave back to his master and thus supporting the evils of slavery.

It would be useless to try to defend Paul for this omission, but several explanations have been offered that help us understand the situation. (*a*) Paul was most concerned here about the welfare of an individual person whom he was putting in great danger by sending him back to his master. An attack upon the institution of slavery in such circumstances could only harm his appeal. Everything is subordinated here to the welfare of the individual, a fact that should not surprise those acquainted with the ministry of Jesus. (*b*) Paul was still convinced that Jesus would return and make earthly institutions such as marriage and slavery irrelevant. (*c*) By attacking slavery, Paul would have brought Christianity into severe danger as a subversive movement. (*d*) Most important of all, Paul established a new relationship between masters and their slaves, a relationship based upon Christian love. Thus he did not openly attack slavery, but planted the seeds of love and justice that made its downfall inevitable.

3. Outline

1. Greeting (vs. 1–3)
2. Gratitude for Philemon (vs. 4–7)
3. Appeal on behalf of Onesimus (vs. 8–22)
4. Farewell (vs. 23–25)

Chapter 10

Philippians

1. Background

Paul's last letter from prison was written to the first church he had founded in Europe. It was also the church strongest in loyalty to him and deepest in his affections. How appropriate it is that the last words we have from him are words of joy and encouragement to people whom he deeply loved!

Philippi was an important city in Macedonia, originally founded as a military settlement by the Romans. For some reason Paul had particular success in proclaiming the gospel in this area, and the church he established had taken deep root. Its members were particularly generous, sending money to their apostle at Thessalonica, his next stopping place after leaving Philippi, and on many other occasions. During one period of hardship in Corinth, Paul received money from them, and because he felt so close to them he broke his own rule about accepting outside financial help. He knew the Philippians would never accuse him of selfish motives.

As soon as these friends heard that Paul had been arrested they hastened to his aid, knowing that prisoners received few comforts and courtesies. Anxious to minister to his needs quickly in this new crisis, they sent a gift with Epaphroditus, one of their members, who had been instructed to stay at Paul's side, assisting him in every possible way. Unfortunately, Epaphroditus had become seriously ill and almost died. Now, fully recovered, he was anxious to return to his friends in Philippi. Paul sends him on his way with a warm and affectionate note, expressing gratitude for their generosity and commending Epaphroditus for his faithfulness.

The letter was written toward the close of Paul's Roman imprisonment, which ended either in A.D. 62 or 64. It is an informal letter written for the *purpose* of expressing gratitude and encouragement to friends of long standing. Because it is so disorderly in its organization, some scholars have doubted its authenticity. Paul jumps from personal greetings to warnings about his enemies, to words of encouragement, to warm expressions of gratitude. It is not at all unusual, however, for a man composing an informal letter to skip about in this way, writing down his thoughts as they occur to him. There is no real ground for doubting the authenticity of this letter on the basis of its poor organization. This is just what we might expect under the circumstances.

One central theme of great significance dominates the entire letter — Christian joy. The Philippians had been anxious about Paul as he faced an indefinite imprisonment and possible death. They had been having troubles of their own: persecution at the hands of the pagans, confusion because of false teachers, and dissension among themselves. Paul's chief aim is to encourage them and he does this by striking a note of radiant joy that is evident on every page.

"I thank my God in all my remembrance of you, always in every prayer of mine for you all making my prayer with

joy. . . . What then? Only that in every way, whether in
pretense or in truth, Christ is proclaimed; and in that I
rejoice. Yes, and I shall rejoice. . . . So if there is any en-
couragement in Christ, any incentive of love, any partici-
pation in the Spirit, any affection and sympathy, complete
my joy by being of the same mind. . . . Finally, my breth-
ren, rejoice in the Lord. . . . Therefore, my brethren, whom
I love and long for, my joy and crown, stand firm thus in
the Lord, my beloved. . . . Rejoice in the Lord always;
again I will say, Rejoice."

The crucial thing to note about Paul's joy is its founda-
tion in Jesus Christ. Here is no superficial peace of mind or
positive thinking that we achieve by telling ourselves that
things will turn out for the best. On the contrary, Christian
joy is one of the rich fruits of life in Christ. When we
have discovered and accepted the "one thing needful," joy
is inevitable. This explains why many of the most moving
things Paul said about God the Father and Jesus Christ
are in this letter in which he tries to share deep and holy
joy with his friends. Here, for example, is a clear indication
of the roots of Paul's own joy: "For to me to live is Christ,
and to die is gain. If it is to be life in the flesh, that means
fruitful labor for me. Yet which I shall choose I cannot tell.
I am hard pressed between the two. My desire is to de-
part and be with Christ, for that is far better" (Phil.
1:21–23).

This is also the letter that contains Paul's moving state-
ment about the selflessness of Christ, "who, though he was
in the form of God, did not count equality with God a
thing to be grasped, but emptied himself, taking the form
of a servant, being born in the likeness of men. . . . There-
fore God has highly exalted him and bestowed on him the
name which is above every name" (Phil. 2:6–7, 9). This
passage has been called "the glory of Philippians." No-

where else in his epistles does Paul rise to loftier heights of eloquence or penetrate deeper into the true nature of Christ. Yet even here he has a specific purpose in mind. Concerned about dissensions in the church, he tries to help the Philippians rise above petty feuds and jealousies by reminding them of the sacrifice of Jesus Christ, who, possessing everything, had surrendered all in unlimited obedience to God. How can those who claim to be his followers allow themselves to get bogged down in pettiness and selfishness? In typical fashion, Paul addresses himself to a particular situation and plumbs the depths of Christian experience at the same time. The problem of Christ's "nature" has been hotly debated for centuries, but Paul's insight has never been surpassed. The secret of Christ's nature, he insists, is found in his selfless submission to God on behalf of men.

As previously indicated, this letter to the best loved of all his churches is probably Paul's farewell utterance. This poignant fact adds to the significance of his glowing words. Facing imminent danger, Christ's apostle shares with his beloved friends the deep and holy joy he has known in Jesus Christ, a joy that is beyond sorrow, beyond suffering, and beyond death. Paul, the restless Hebrew of Hebrews who first found Christ in a blinding light on the open road, was nearing the end of his long journey. Like Christ, he never had anyplace "to lay his head," for he was constantly moving about, spreading the good news, sharing his joy, proclaiming the new life with God in Christ. But now the mission was accomplished, the journey ended, and with it the danger, the toil and hardship, the sleepless nights, and the anxiety for his churches. His desire to depart and be with Christ was soon to be realized, and so he leaves his final word: "Rejoice in the Lord always; again I will say, Rejoice."

2. Problems

The chief problem in Philippians arises when we try to explain the passage in which Paul attacks the false teachers (Phil. 3:2 to 4:1). His change of mood is so abrupt that it defies explanation, suddenly shifting from warmth and friendliness to anger and vehemence. The bitterness of his attack is unsurpassed even in Galatians. "Look out for the dogs, look out for the evil-workers, look out for those who mutilate the flesh."

Some attempts have been made to explain this break by insisting that we have the fragments of two letters in our present Philippians. Others are convinced that this passage has been interpolated from some other letter. Such arguments are not convincing, because in many other places in the letter Paul turns sharply from one subject to another. Writing informally to friends, he does not bother with any principle of organization. It certainly would be in character for him to turn abruptly and unexpectedly on false teachers, attacking them vigorously because of the damage they were doing to his "children in Christ." We know from his other letters how strenuously he opposed such "enemies." It is therefore safe to believe in the essential unity of this letter, attributing its disorganization to the situation out of which it arose.

3. Outline

1. Greetings in Christ (ch. 1:1–11)
2. Paul's joy in Christ (ch. 1:12–26)
3. Encouragement and appeal (chs. 1:27 to 2:18)
4. Personal matters (chs. 2:19 to 3:1)
5. Warning against false teachers (chs. 3:2 to 4:1)
6. Final appeal and farewell (ch. 4:2–23)

Chapter 11

Ephesians

1. Background

THE LETTER to the Ephesians has been praised as "one
of the divinest compositions of man," a work of depth
and beauty, "carrying us to the highest pinnacles of Chris-
tian speculation with a daring that is matched only by its
reverence and humility." Much of its language has passed
into the life of the church in prayers, hymns, and liturgies.
One of our richest records of Christian experience, it has
served the spiritual needs of countless persons and con-
tributed profound insights to Christian theology.

It is at the same time a book that presents the student
with the most serious and baffling problems. Until the
nineteenth century it was assumed that it was written by
Paul to the church in Ephesus during his imprisonment in
Rome. The majority of scholars are now convinced that it
was not written by Paul, nor was it sent to the Ephesians.
It is usually dated near the end of the first century, though
there is very little agreement on the matter of chronology.
Even more perplexing is the wide variety of interpretations
given to the contents of the book. We can't even agree on
the author's purpose in writing!

As far as authorship is concerned, Paul is mentioned at least twice in the letter, along with Tychicus, who took Paul's letter from Rome to the Colossians. Early in the nineteenth century, however, serious questions were raised about the authenticity of the letter and a considerable amount of evidence has been compiled that throws doubt on the Pauline authorship. The style is unlike any of the apostle's other letters, moving in long and involved sentences completely different from the impetuous movement characteristic of his thought. The language, which is wordy and heavy, includes many terms that do not appear elsewhere in Paul's writing, nor anywhere else in the New Testament, for that matter. Even when Paul's words and ideas appear in this letter, they are used in a new and radically different way. We may add to this evidence the fact that Paul is highly praised in this letter, but in other places he tells how "foolish" he feels when commending himself. Finally, the book contains many signs of a highly developed church life, including the veneration of prophets and apostles as the foundation of the church. Paul, on the other hand, had always insisted that Christ is the church's one foundation.

For these and other reasons, it is now widely believed that Ephesians was written by a brilliant follower of Paul, one who was thoroughly acquainted with Paul's writings and perhaps with Paul himself. He wrote the letter as a tribute of love and admiration, using Paul's name because he knew how indebted he was to the apostle for ideas that he now developed in his own way. Those who wish to verify this indebtedness are urged to compare Ephesians with Colossians and discover how often this writer has borrowed ideas and exact phrases.

Even more certain is the current belief that the letter was not written to the Ephesians. The author clearly states that it is a general letter written to all believers: "To the saints who are also faithful in Christ Jesus." The words "in Ephesus" do not appear in any Greek manuscript before the fourth century and are obviously a scribal insertion. More convincing evidence may be found in the tone of the letter. Paul had worked for three years in Ephesus and had made countless friends, but unlike his other letters, Ephesians does not include personal greetings to a single individual. He implies, too, that the readers of the letter have never seen him or heard him personally. He tells them, "I have heard of your faith." Would he write in this way to friends with whom he had lived and labored for over three years?

We conclude, therefore, that Ephesians was written by a gifted and devoted follower of Paul as a general letter to all Christians or perhaps as a "cover" or introduction to the collected Pauline letters. Historical conditions reflected in the contents lead us to date it about A.D. 85–95. Recognizing a wide difference of opinion among interpreters, we may state the main *purpose* as follows: to show how the supremacy of Jesus Christ makes possible the fulfillment of God's plan for the unity of all things. Paul's ideas on the supremacy and uniqueness of Christ, stated most clearly in Colossians, have been taken over by this author and developed into a Christian philosophy of history.

Early in the letter we are made to realize that the universe is now in a tragic state of endless discord, strife, division, and conflict. Elements in the world of nature are in conflict with one another, persons cannot seem to live in harmony with one another, even families and houses are divided against themselves. Far worse, there is growing strife in the church caused by growing doctrinal disputes that give rise to divisive sects and parties. The problem of discord in the church, that Paul had faced in Corinth, increased rather than diminished as the church expanded. This became progressively more serious, for a divided church could hardly hope to survive the mounting attacks of Rome. "Unite or perish" was a challenge the church could not escape.

In the midst of all this confusion, the author of Ephesians discerns a secret divine plan, a "mystery" of creation now made plain through Jesus Christ. "For he has made known to us in all wisdom and insight the mystery of his will, according to his purpose which he set forth in Christ as a plan for the fullness of time, to unite all things in him, things in heaven and things on earth." (Eph. 1:9–10.) Specifically, God's plan is for all the discordant elements in the universe to move toward unity in Jesus Christ. A sign of this unity is found in the fellowship of Jews and Gentiles already accomplished in the church, and in the reconciliation already accomplished among former enemies, but this is only a pledge of things to come.

We may call Ephesians a Christian philosophy of history because of the author's conviction that the meaning of all history must be read in terms of God's plan for unity through Jesus Christ.

Scholars have long puzzled over the close relation of Ephesians to Paul's letter to the Colossians. This is not difficult to understand when we remember that Paul's purpose in writing had been to combat a heresy that attempted to make Christ one among many mediators between God and man. In opposition, Paul had emphasized the absolute supremacy and uniqueness of Christ. The writer to the Ephesians now lifts this idea out of its earlier context and applies it to the wider problems of human history. He believed that he had found in this letter the real key to Paul's thought and to the mystery of the universe, so he used it more than any other Pauline writings in the composition of his own letter.

Running throughout the author's argument is his conviction that God's instrument in achieving harmony and unity among men is the church of Jesus Christ. His appreciation for the church as the "one" body of Christ was extremely influential in later Christian thought. Christ and the church here constitute a union as real as the union between personality and body in an individual, the church thus serving as the organism through which Christ manifests himself in the world. This was the basis of later supernatural claims on the part of church leaders, climaxing in the belief that outside of the church there is no salvation.

The church in the writer's own time represented for him the primary stage in the great unifying purpose of God for the whole creation. Until Christ came, Jews and Gentiles were divided. But Christ broke down the wall of partition, making possible in the church the union of Jews and Gentiles. Amazing as this new unity is, it is only a sign of things to come when all of humanity will be brought into the one body of Christ to live in a spirit of love, harmony, and obedience to the Holy God.

Finally, it should be noted how the language and style of Ephesians support the main argument by cultivating a feeling of reverence for Christ and for the God whose grace is now offered to men through Christ. The book is written in the form of a prayer or devotional meditation in which even the deepest religious ideas are clothed in a style that borders on the sublime. The opening hymn of adoration moves immediately into a prayer for spiritual enlightenment. The mighty acts of God in Christ are recounted in a way that moves the reader to praise God rather than to question or challenge. Another magnificent prayer, seeking all the fullness of God for the reader, suddenly breaks into a doxology: "Now to him who by the power at work within us is able to do far more abundantly than all that we ask or think, to him be glory in the church

and in Christ Jesus to all generations, for ever and ever.
Amen" (Eph. 3:20–21). Constant reference is made to the
wonder of salvation by faith: "For by grace you have been
saved through faith; and this is not your own doing, it is
the gift of God" (Eph. 2:8). Even the moral exhortation of
the last three chapters is presented in the language of
prayer and devotion. It is no surprise that the language of
Ephesians has appeared so often in the worship of the
church, nor is it any wonder that we are moved to glorify
God as we read it.

2. *Problems*

We have already indicated the many serious difficulties
that plague those who attempt to interpret this book intel-
ligently. The problem of authenticity is the most serious,
however, and the possibility of Pauline authorship cannot
be lightly dismissed. It is possible that Paul repeated in this
letter some of the ideas of his former letters, changing his
style and tone because he was writing for a more general
situation. It has also been pointed out as "almost convinc-
ing," that an imitator is always inferior to his model.
Ephesians is such a creative work it is impossible to believe
that in the early church there was an unknown teacher of
such excellence.

The weight of evidence in the other direction is even
more convincing, however, as we have attempted to show.
Differences in language and style are so great that it is ex-
tremely difficult to believe that one man could be respon-
sible for both Ephesians and Colossians. The ideas are defi-
nitely Pauline, but they are applied and developed in an
entirely new way. Nor can we overlook the letter's venera-
tion of Paul, the prophets, and the apostles, an attitude
quite indicative of a time late in the first century. In an-
swer to the "convincing" argument above, we know of sev-

eral great unknown teachers in the early church, including the authors of Hebrews and the Fourth Gospel. Why not also for this baffling and inspiring letter to the Ephesians?

3. Outline

1. Greeting (ch. 1:1–2)
2. The unity of all things in Christ (chs. 1:3 to 3:21)
   a. The theme (ch. 1:3–14)
   b. Prayer for spiritual enlightenment (chs. 1:15 to 2:10)
   c. Jews and Gentiles united through Christ (chs. 2:11 to 3:13)
   d. Doxology (ch. 3:14–21)
3. Ethical teaching (chs. 4:1 to 6:20)
   a. Unity in the church (ch. 4:1–16)
   b. Rejection of pagan life (chs. 4:17 to 5:20)
   c. Unity in the family (chs. 5:21 to 6:9)
   d. The armor of God (ch. 6:10–20)
4. Farewell (ch. 6:21–24)

Chapter 12

The Pastoral Letters

1. Background

THE LETTERS to Timothy and Titus are the only books in the New Testament written primarily for Christian ministers. Pastoral letters, messages sent by church leaders to Christian pastors and their "flocks," have been an important form of communication in the life of the church, but none are more important than these three earliest ones. All were written by the same hand and reflect a similar situation. An identical purpose runs through them all, and similar religious ideas and language appear throughout. For these reasons, they are ordinarily considered and interpreted together as a unit or group.

The letters have come down to us under the name of Paul, who addresses them to his two younger missionary companions, Timothy and Titus, giving them instructions for their work as busy pastors. But scholars are now almost unanimous in doubting the Pauline authorship of these documents for reasons that fall under five general headings: (a) historical data; (b) language and style; (c) religious ideas; (d) ecclesiastical organization; (e) second-century heresies. Because of the bearing that the problem of authorship has upon the interpretation of these letters, careful consideration must be given to the available evidence.

Most of the historical data at our disposal leads us to believe that Paul's Roman imprisonment ended with his condemnation and death. The book of The Acts breaks off before arriving at this point in his career, but the earliest traditions support this conclusion. There are some who believe that Paul, acquitted in his first trial, carried on a missionary campaign in Spain and returned to Rome where he was tried, condemned, and executed. But the lack of evidence in support of such a position is very troubling, since we surely would have heard something of his activity in Spain if he had worked there. The pastoral letters all assume a very different situation in Paul's life from any that we know about in our present records. They could have been written only in the period between his trial and death in Rome, but there is no reasonable ground to believe that such an interval of missionary activity actually took place.

In language and style, these three letters are very similar to one another but entirely unlike anything we have from the hand of Paul. Many important words and phrases that occur throughout the letters appear nowhere in Paul or in the rest of the New Testament. More obvious to the casual reader is the difference in mood and style. The emotional intensity, the flashes of brilliance, and the deep spiritual insight that we have come to associate with Paul are all missing. By contrast, this author's style is slow, repetitious, diffuse, and even tedious at times. It is impossible to conceive of Paul changing so completely in his last years that he lost the spark of communication that makes his other letters so moving and memorable.

Certainly the most striking and significant difference be-

tween these pastoral letters and the letters of Paul is the
contrast in religious ideas. For Paul, faith had been a vital
inner experience by which we accept the grace of God in
Christ and become "new creatures," living a new life of
love and spiritual power. Faith, from the human stand-
point, is a matter of absolute trust and confidence in God
the Father, whose love has now become known through
Jesus Christ. For the author of the pastoral letters, faith is
something quite different, less a matter of trust and more a
matter of belief. His interest is in *the* faith, a body of doc-
trines that determine the standard for entrance into the
church. For this reason, he does not see the vital relation-
ship between faith and the ethical life of the individual
that Paul had stressed so often. On the contrary, this
author exhorts his readers to believe sound doctrine and
live a good life, never relating the two. This serious weak-
ening of Christian experience can hardly be attributed to
Paul, who understood so well the deeper meaning of
Christ-centered faith and love.

There are also in these letters many signs of an advanced
ecclesiastical organization entirely unknown during Paul's
life and ministry. In earlier days there was no official minis-
try, but only "Spirit led" apostles and prophets, who
moved from place to place, baptizing converts and gather-
ing them into communities of faith. The author of these
letters gives evidence of a later situation by taking it for
granted that his readers are familiar with bishops, elders,
and deacons. The church organization has been stabilized
by means of "ordained" ministers all working under a hier-
archical organization whose purpose is to maintain and
transmit the "true faith." Such an advanced state of affairs,
entirely unknown to Paul, reflects a much later period in
the life of the church.

Finally, there are many indications in these letters of
highly developed second-century heresies that were threat-

ening the existence of the church. The false teachers against whom Paul had written in Colossians were forerunners of others who tried to lead Christianity into all kinds of doctrinal and ethical blind alleys. Early in the second century these became such a serious threat that the church had to gather all of its strength to combat them. Almost every paragraph in these pastoral letters reflects this situation. The false teachers are denounced as corrupt, depraved, vain, ignorant, deceivers, and liars. They are "lovers of self, lovers of money, proud, arrogant, abusive, disobedient to their parents, ungrateful, unholy, inhuman, implacable, slanderers, profligates, fierce, haters of good, treacherous, reckless, swollen with conceit, lovers of pleasure rather than lovers of God, holding the form of religion but denying the power of it" (II Tim. 3:2–5). There have been a great many scholarly attempts to identify these "enemies of Christ," but without much success. The direct and indirect references seem to reflect the entire rampant sectarian movement of the early decades of the second century, which forced the church to consolidate its beliefs and strengthen its structure and organization.

For all these reasons, the Pauline authorship of these letters is now almost wholly discounted. This does not crowd Paul entirely out of the picture, however, nor does it account for many passages in the letters that sound very much like Paul. It has been suggested that this author has taken genuine Pauline fragments, short notes that Paul had written to his assistants, and has used them as a core around which he wrote a larger work. For this reason, and because he sincerely believed that he was expressing the "mind of Paul" for the second century, he issued the letters under Paul's name. We may therefore regard them as "Pauline" to some degree, even though not written by the great apostle himself.

We can now say with relative certainty that the pas-

toral letters were written by an unknown author greatly
influenced by Paul, who wrote during the early decades of
the second century (A.D. 100–150), probably from Rome
where the heretical sects were causing so much trouble.
His *purpose* is to combat the growing heresies of his time
by setting forth the qualifications and duties of Christian
pastors. Uppermost in the writer's mind is the primary
duty of every pastor, which he considers to be the defense
and transmission of sound doctrine. More than any other
document in the New Testament, these letters are con-
cerned with the establishment of Christian orthodoxy.
They speak time and again of sound doctrine and sound
teaching as if there is already a body of "truth" that is
standard or orthodox for Christian believers. Because a
pastor's first duty is the transmission of such truth, he
must, of course, be orthodox himself, following "the pat-
tern of sound words," "rightly handling the word of truth."

The letters taken together emphasize four functions of
the ministry that are especially important in view of
threats from heretical sects: (*a*) The orthodox faith must
be preached with vigor and enthusiasm. Such labor will
leave no time for vain speculation and agitation over myths
and pagan philosophy. (*b*) Church leaders must be chosen
with the greatest care if orthodoxy is to be maintained.
For this reason, a great deal of guidance is offered in these
letters to those responsible for choosing leaders and "laying
on hands" in ordination. (*c*) Discipline must be main-
tained among the ministers, who should "set the believers
an example in speech and conduct, in love, in faith, in
purity." Rules are given for the punishment and exclusion
of those who persist in sin or "wrong thinking." (*d*) The
worship of the community must be carefully controlled in
form and content. Prayer is emphasized as well as the ex-
planation of Scripture through preaching and teaching.

Women may attend public worship inconspicuously and in silence, but they are not to preach or lead in prayer.

Through all of this we detect a deep earnestness and a commendable sense of dedication to the Christian movement. The author finds the church of his time locked in a death struggle with strong and vigorous opponents. Not a creative and original thinker himself, he was a fanatically loyal churchman who saw the necessity of maintaining the faith with resolute courage. He was also an able administrator, believing firmly that Christians must be well-organized to withstand attacks from their enemies. In writing about these problems, he describes the ideals of the Christian life in an impressive and practical way.

Having said this, however, we must point out that most readers find the impact of these letters disappointingly below that of most of the New Testament. Only rarely do they approach the level of inspiration and spiritual insight achieved by Paul, the great apostle whose name they bear. On some of the most important matters, such as faith and ethics, they miss the Pauline spirit entirely.

We cannot emphasize too strongly the contrast between Paul and the pastoral letters at this point. For the great apostle, faith had been a dynamic inward experience, a union with Christ that enabled a man to enter into a new kind of relationship with God. It was an experience of confident trust in the grace of God and in the good news of God's forgiving love now available to men through Jesus Christ. There is a warmth, a sense of reality, and a life-transforming quality about Paul's conception of faith that is totally missing from the pastoral letters. Faith here, as we have indicated, is merely the acceptance of a set of beliefs and principles that has been handed down from the past. A Christian is no longer one who has entered into a new kind of relationship with God through faith in Christ, but one who believes the right things! Here is the difference between dynamic and static religion in clear and bold outline.

Just as he misses the deeper meaning of Christian faith, so the author fails to see the essential connection between faith and the Christian life. Paul had insisted that the Christian life grows out of a person's new life in Christ as inevitably as fruit grows on a healthy tree. Those who become new creatures in Christ begin to live a new kind of life because of the religious experience they have had. In the pastoral letters no such connection is drawn. The author emphasizes good works in a moralizing way, exhorting people to do good deeds that will be acceptable to God. The exact opposite of the approach taken in Paul and the Gospels, this concept misses the uniqueness of the Christian ethic entirely.

From the beginning, the organized church has been plagued by a tendency toward formalism and externalism. The warmth of faith as a living relationship with God through Christ is too often replaced by the coldness of creeds and catechisms. Too many persons think of certain beliefs rather than newness of life in Christ as the standard for church membership. Christian preaching, originally the proclamation of incredible good news, degenerates into the lifeless application of moral discipline. Christians tend to become Pharisees. In view of these facts, the greatest value of the pastoral letters is in warning the church against that kind of static and unimaginative religion which becomes the enemy of Christ in every generation.

2. Problems

The greatest problem of these documents is that of authorship. We have already discussed the matter in some detail, but it should be noted that an amazing amount of scholarly attention has been devoted to this issue in the last century. Books have been published on the relation of these letters to second-century heresies. Words and ideas have been analyzed, counted, and compared. We have suggested the overwhelming majority opinion, but there are still a few conservative scholars who cling to the theory of Pauline authorship.

Equally difficult, though not so important, are the problems of date and place of composition. Some hold that the letters were written near the beginning of the second century; others find evidence of mid-second-century sects and beliefs. We are relatively safe, therefore, in choosing a date with a broad range of possibilities, A.D. 100–150. We have suggested that the letters were written from Rome, but some scholars insist that the problems reflect the church in Asia, particularly Ephesus, and such a view cannot be wholly discounted. Once again we see that there is no sure and easy way to recover the past. Our search for truth, like faith itself, is a dynamic and growing experience.

3. Outline

FIRST TIMOTHY

1. Greetings (ch. 1:1–2)
2. The importance of sound doctrine (ch. 1:3–20)
3. Rules for church life (chs. 2:1 to 3:16)
   a. Prayer and worship (ch. 2:1–15)
   b. Church organization (ch. 3:1–16)
4. Rules for the pastor (chs. 4:1 to 6:21)
   a. Toward various persons (chs. 4:1 to 6:19)
   b. Closing advice (ch. 6:20–21)

SECOND TIMOTHY

1. Greeting and thanksgiving (chs. 1:1 to 2:13)
2. Attack on the heretics (chs. 2:14 to 3:9)

3. The necessity of orthodoxy (chs. 3:10 to 4:8)
4. Personal note and farewell (ch. 4:9–22)

TITUS

1. Greeting (ch. 1:1–4)
2. Rules for church leaders (ch. 1:5–16)
3. Rules for the Christian life (chs. 2:1 to 3:11)
4. Personal note and farewell (ch. 3:12–15)

Chapter 13

Hebrews

1. Background

IN MANY modern cities, the Christian church is the easiest organization for a person to join. A signature on a registration card and a handshake with the pastor are often the sole requirements for membership. For this reason, it is almost impossible for us to understand a book like Hebrews, written for persons who were in imminent danger of losing their possessions and their lives simply because they belonged to the church.

The dangers were particularly great in Rome, the capital of the Empire. In that terrible August of A.D. 64, Nero tried to lay the blame for the burning of the city upon the Christians. As a result they were hunted down and killed, often as objects of amusement and sport for the pagan Romans. Tacitus, the ancient historian, describes how "they were covered with the hides of wild beasts and worried to death by dogs, or nailed to crosses or set fire to, and when day declined burned to serve for nocturnal lights. Nero offered his own gardens for the spectacle." Through all such persecutions the Roman Christians had remained strong and faithful, but the end was not yet in sight. As they approached the close of the first century, more persecutions were threatening, and with them, more of the sufferings echoed in Hebrews: "Some were tortured. . . . Others suffered mocking and scourging. . . . They were stoned, they were sawn in two, they were killed with the sword."

Only strong Christians could withstand such an attack, persons sustained by a glowing experience of the gospel that led them to look upon their relation to God through Christ as the most important thing in life, more important than life itself! But unfortunately most of the Christians in the Roman church by A.D. 80–90 were second- and third-generation Christians. They had grown up in the faith, and, never knowing any other, were taking it for granted. They were Christians as a matter of custom and not of conviction. Adding to the general apathy permeating the church was the discouragement of continuous persecutions and the dimming of hopes for the Lord's return. The author of Hebrews, keenly aware of what another major persecution might do to a spiritually weakened church, wrote an eloquent and persuasive declaration of Christian faith. His pervading desire throughout the entire work is to rekindle the glow of enthusiasm that had made it possible for the earlier generations to withstand the terrible persecution from the enemies of Christ.

Apart from this general purpose, we know very little about The Letter to the Hebrews. Among the many riddles surrounding it is the fact that it is not a letter, nor was it written to Hebrews. Although often studied in relation to the Pauline letters, it was most certainly not written by Paul. We have already suggested that it was composed for the Christians in Rome about A.D. 80–90, but these facts cannot be established with absolute certainty. In addition to these difficulties it should be noted that this is probably the least known of all New Testament writings in our own time because of its complex and archaic language.

In spite of all these problems, however, the book merits careful study as a moving manifesto of faith.

Although Hebrews has been traditionally ascribed to Paul, there are no reasonable grounds for believing that he actually wrote it. The differences are so great in style, form, and content that some interpreters doubt whether the author knew anything of the teaching of Paul. The fact that the apostle did not write it was fully recognized in the early church, and in the second and third centuries many attempts were made to guess at the authorship. Luke, Clement of Rome, and Barnabas were suggested. Martin Luther believed that it was written by Apollos, whom the book of The Acts describes as an Alexandrian, "an eloquent man, well versed in the scriptures." Perhaps Origen, the greatest of the early critics, is the most discerning when he suggests that the "author is known to God alone." All we can say is that he was a great unknown, a brilliant teacher, eloquent in speech, and highly trained in the use of Scripture.

Other matters of historical importance are not quite so obscure. It seems relatively certain that the "letter" was sent to Christians in Rome. Clement of Rome, writing before the end of the first century, quotes it extensively. The book itself contains the words "Those who come from Italy send you greetings." This implies that a Roman church leader temporarily outside Italy sends greetings along with other Italian Christians. The document reflects a type of thinking prevalent in the latter part of the first century and seems to be written against the background of the persecutions under Domitian, emperor from A.D. 81 to 96. We have suggested, therefore, a date of A.D. 80–90.

The author's *purpose*, stated above in general terms, is to rekindle the faith of the Christian community by emphasizing Christianity as the absolute religion that gives men direct access to the living God. He assumes throughout his argument: (a) that all men long to realize the presence of God and (b) that religions may be judged by their ability to satisfy this longing. Christianity is the absolute religion because it satisfies man's longing for God "absolutely." Jesus Christ has opened a "new and living way" to God.

The author works from a two-story view of the universe, the lower story made up of transient, material things, the upper story of eternal, spiritual things. The goal of man's life is to grasp eternal realities, to live above the world of fleeting ephemeral shadows that we see around us. "By faith," we grasp the higher realities, discovering as we do that the Holy God is the supreme reality of this "other" world. Religion at its best enables man to lay hold of eternal things, and ultimately to apprehend God, the supreme reality, "the Majesty in heaven."

Because Judaism, next to Christianity, has been the most successful in achieving this purpose, the writer sets out to show how Christianity surpasses Judaism. For him, the religion of Israel centered in the high priest who renewed the people's covenant with God on the Day of Atonement. Once a year he offered a sacrifice for the sins of the people and then carried the blood of the sacrifice through the veil into the Holy of Holies where he stood in the presence of God. As representative of the people, he thus atoned for their sins and renewed the solemn covenant with God for another year. This was the most effective religion prior to Christianity, but now that Christ has come we see that even Judaism was but a foreshadow of something higher to come.

In this higher religion, Jesus Christ is the supreme High Priest who identifies himself completely with men, yet owes his appointment and authority to God alone. He did not owe his priesthood to physical descent, but was a priest "after the order of Melchizedek," whose authority rested on the power of his own life. As the true High Priest, Christ offered a supreme sacrifice for man's sins — his own life. Then, with the blood of this incomparable sacrifice, he lifted the veil between earth and heaven and entered directly into the presence of God where he remains forever. His continuous intercession for us means that we have access to God, not just once a year through the power of another, but continually and directly. Thus Christ has opened the way for men to enter the presence of God and satisfy the deepest hunger of their existence. This is the author's main point, as he directly states: "Now the point in what we are saying is this: we have such a high priest, one who is seated at the right hand of the throne of the Majesty in heaven, a minister in the sanctuary and the true tent which is set up not by man but by the Lord" (Heb. 8:1–2).

The whole book is built around this argument. The early passages (Heb., chs. 1 to 4) lead into the discussion of Christ as the true High Priest by showing how he is higher than prophets, angels, and lawgivers. The main argument is developed in a great central section (Heb., chs. 5 to 10) that is followed by practical exhortation stressing the higher obligations demanded by the absolute religion (Heb., chs. 11 to 13).

The eleventh chapter, the most famous in the book, is often isolated by modern readers, but it grows out of the central argument. It is a hymn in praise of faith that is "the assurance of things hoped for, the conviction of things not seen." By this the author simply means that faith is the power within us to rise above our transient material world and grasp unseen realities. The exciting thing about all the persons in the roll call of witnesses is that they achieved greatness by just such faith, many of them giving up their lives in loyalty to values seen only dimly and from afar. But if their example moves us, how much more we

ought to lay aside the weight of sin and run with per-
severance the race that is set before us, "looking to Jesus
the pioneer and perfecter of our faith, who for the joy that
was set before him endured the cross, despising the shame,
and is seated at the right hand of the throne of God" (Heb.
12:2).

One other facet of the writer's thought should be men-
tioned because of the influence it has had on later Christian
thought. Christ's humanity is emphasized in an eloquent
way during the argument that shows how the true High
Priest has identified himself with his people. "In the days
of his flesh, Jesus offered up prayers and supplications,
with loud cries and tears, to him who was able to save him
from death, and he was heard for his godly fear. . . . For
we have not a high priest who is unable to sympathize with
our weaknesses, but one who in every respect has been
tempted as we are, yet without sinning. Let us then with
confidence draw near to the throne of grace, that we may
receive mercy and find grace to help in time of need."
(Heb. 5:7; 4:15–16.) This emphasis is in sharp contrast
to Paul's intention "not to know Christ after the flesh."
Outside of the Gospels, The Letter to the Hebrews is the
New Testament document that most clearly grasps the
full significance of Christ's earthly life, apart from which
he would be neither our true High Priest nor our Savior.

2. Problems

We have already indicated many of the problems in-
volved in the study of Hebrews, problems which, for the
most part, must remain unsolved. Even the form of the
book is confusing. Because it closes in epistolary style with
personal notices and greetings, it is known as a "letter" to
the Hebrews. But it opens like a theological discourse, and
at many points the writer makes it clear that he is thinking

of himself as a speaker before an audience. Perhaps the teacher who wrote it intended it to be read aloud as a speech, but concluded it like a letter, since he was writing from a distance.

The book has been widely praised for its highly polished literary style, but this is obscured for the modern reader because of our unfamiliarity with Greek and because the sacrificial and priestly terminology is alien to our experience. The latter factor, one of the most serious weaknesses of the book, accounts for its archaic atmosphere. The author did not have Paul's ability to lift eternal truths out of their immediate context and make them relevant for all time. But those who are patient enough to master the unfamiliar language soon discover why The Letter to the Hebrews has always been counted among the most significant of Christian writings. Its pages lift us up into that realm of eternal reality where the person and work of Jesus Christ make it possible for us to enter by "a new and living way" into the presence of God.

3. *Outline*

1. Prelude: the superiority of Jesus (chs. 1:1 to 4:13)
   a. Superior to prophets (ch. 1:1–3)
   b. Superior to angels (chs. 1:4 to 2:18)
   c. Superior to Moses (chs. 3:1 to 4:13)
2. Main argument: Jesus as the true High Priest (chs. 4:14 to 10:39)
   a. A better priesthood (chs. 4:14 to 7:28)
   b. A better covenant (chs. 8:1 to 9:10)
   c. A better sacrifice (chs. 9:11 to 10:39)
3. Postlude: practical exhortation (chs. 11:1 to 13:25)
   a. Example of the faithful (ch. 11:1–40)
   b. Warning and encouragement (ch. 12:1–29)
   c. Practical advice (ch. 13:1–25)

Chapter 14

The Gospel of Mark

1. Background

THE FOUR Gospels are the best-known books in the New Testament. Not only do they appear first in order, but they contain practically all that we know of the life and teaching of Jesus. They are not biographies in a strict sense, but "evangelical biographies," a new kind of literature. Their main purpose is to proclaim the "good news" of God's saving act in Jesus Christ. Each of them handles the historical and biographical material differently, each arises out of a different situation, but all are aimed at setting forth the glad tidings of God's mighty act in Christ.

The Gospels appear first in the New Testament, even though they are later in date than many of the other books. They deserve this priority because of their accounts of the ministry of Jesus and because they are based on documents and traditions that reach back to the earliest times. Since all of the New Testament writings grew out of experiences that came to men through the Christ-event, it was perfectly natural to put those documents first that reported the event itself, particularly in view of the fact that they reached back to actual eyewitnesses and participants for their information. This reliance upon early sources strengthens the priority rights of the Gospels, even though they did not appear in their present form until forty or more years after the events they describe.

The Gospels need to be studied together because of similarities in content and general purpose. They also need to be examined separately, because each has a particular purpose and character of its own. Although many casual readers tend to merge the four Gospel accounts into one picture of Jesus, each writer has looked at his subject from a distinct point of view and thus makes a uniquely valuable contribution to our knowledge of Jesus. Most of Mark's Gospel, for example, is included in Matthew and Luke, but we would never think of dispensing with Mark. Among other things: (*a*) it is closely related to Peter, the "prince of apostles"; (*b*) it was written for the benefit of those about to suffer martyrdom; and (*c*) it is the earliest Gospel. All these factors must be given due consideration in any study of the Gospel of Mark.

When Peter died, the early church lost one of its most important sources of information about Jesus. The strong and impetuous apostle who had been very close to Jesus had become one of the great leaders in the world-wide mission of the church. As we might expect, he had traveled tirelessly, talking about the events in Jesus' life and explaining his teaching. But now Peter was dead, and unless someone thought to write down what he could remember of Peter's words, a priceless treasury of knowledge about Jesus would be lost forever. Fortunately there was such a person, as we discover in the testimony of Papias, a bishop of the early church who wrote about A.D. 140:

This also the presbyter used to say: "Mark, indeed, who became the interpreter of Peter, wrote accurately, as far

as he remembered them, the things said or done by the
Lord, but not however in order." For he [Mark] had
neither heard the Lord nor been his personal follower, but
at a later stage, as I said, he had followed Peter, who
used to adapt the teachings to the needs of the moment,
but not as though he were drawing up a connected ac-
count of the oracles of the Lord: so that Mark committed
no error in writing certain matters just as he remembered
them. For he had only one object in view, namely, to leave
out nothing of the things which he had heard, and to in-
clude no false statement among them. (Eusebius, *Church
History*, III.39.15.)

Scholars cannot agree on certain aspects of this report, but
most accept the general tradition that this Gospel is closely
related to Peter through Mark, his companion and inter-
preter.

John Mark was a Jew of Jerusalem whose mother's
house had been a place of prayer in the early days of the
church. We do not know when he was converted, but we
find much evidence of his missionary activity as a com-
panion of Barnabas, Peter, and Paul (Acts 12:25; Col. 4:10;
I Peter 5:13). He had become very familiar with Peter's
preaching while serving as his translator, and he realized
at once the tragic loss if Peter's recollections of Jesus per-
ished. His narrative in its present form is a compilation of
many sources, but it is essentially Peter's picture of Jesus
that he preserves. This reason alone should lead us to rank
this Gospel high among the richest treasures of our reli-
gious heritage.

It is also valuable because it was written for Christians
in Rome who were about to die "for the faith." Peter and
Paul had both perished in Nero's persecution about A.D.
62–64. Countless other Christians were fed to wild animals
and burned alive, and though the persecutions fell off for

a time, they would certainly begin again. Members of the church needed to be strengthened by recalling the good news of Jesus Christ, especially the example of his suffering and death.

The general mood of Mark's Gospel confirms his desire to strengthen persons facing a period of intense crisis. His words are strong and bold as he describes the courage of Jesus in facing suffering and death. As the story moves swiftly and dramatically toward its climax on the cross, Mark heightens the dramatic mood by using the present tense and by repeating his favorite word, "immediately." In this Gospel, Jesus is the man of action constantly moving about, meeting crowds, challenging opponents, proclaiming the good news, and traveling unhesitatingly toward death in Jerusalem while his disciples hang back in fear.

The plan of the Gospel is also intended to emphasize the fearless suffering and death of Jesus. The first half of the book is comprised of a series of somewhat loosely connected stories, but the second half, devoted to the Passion story, hums with excitement. In contrast, Matthew and Luke devote only about one quarter of their books to the Jerusalem ministry. Thus Mark reminds those about to die of the example set for them by their Lord and helps to answer the question that plagued all potential martyrs and all friends of martyrs, Why does God permit those who love him to die for their faith? Mark's Gospel is a portrait of Jesus for an age of crisis.

The fact that this is the earliest Gospel also contributes to its historical value. We cannot determine its precise date of composition, but A.D. 64 may be taken as the earliest possible date, since Peter died about that time. Some scholars, believing that the author knew nothing of the terrible destruction of Jerusalem that occurred in A.D. 70, set the date of the Gospel as A.D. 64–70. Others, however, insist that there are definite references to the fall of the city and the destruction of the Temple (cf. Mark 13:14). This means that the Gospel must have been written in the year A.D. 70, or very shortly thereafter, since it was a well-established work when Matthew and Luke were composed later in the century.

Whichever date is accepted, Mark is still the earliest of the Gospels. In its present form it is a composite work, as Matthew and Luke are, but it takes us very close to Jesus by using the recollections of Peter as its main source. It provides us with our oldest connected account of the ministry and message of Jesus, an account that both Matthew and Luke used in the composition of their Gospels. These later works reflect more obvious concern for historical accuracy, but Mark's chronology and order are almost always trustworthy. Nearly all modern writers follow Mark's general order when attempting to form a coherent account of the life of Jesus. There have been some attempts among modern scholars to establish the primacy of Matthew, but their arguments so far are not convincing. Matthew is first in canonical order, but Mark is first in seniority.

In summary, we may say that Mark's Gospel is a strong and dramatic account of the life of Jesus written about A.D. 70 by John Mark, missionary companion of Peter and Paul. His *purpose* is to preserve Peter's priceless recollections of Jesus in a document that will strengthen Roman Christians facing martyrdom because of their faith.

Those who read the Gospel carefully will notice many characteristics that set it apart from the others. Modern pilgrims to the Holy Land value it highly because it contains the greatest detail of *everyday life* in Palestine: fishermen and their nets, working people in the fields, vineyards, animals, food, and clothes. It is the Gospel most filled with references to the *human traits* of Jesus: he wonders, hungers, pities, groans, fears, prays, and becomes angry and fatigued. It is the most *unpolished* in form, Matthew and Luke often correcting Mark's grammar or using a more appropriate word. Finally, this Gospel is much more concerned with the *life* of Jesus than with his teaching. The two cannot be separated, as Mark recognizes, but we discover in Matthew and Luke how much of the teaching of Jesus has been omitted by Mark in order to emphasize the life of the courageous Son of God.

2. Problems

One of the most serious problems faced by New Testament students is that of tracing the relationship of the four Gospels. All give an account of the life and teaching of Jesus, but serious differences become obvious when we compare them. John's Gospel differs radically from the others in form, content, and style. He often changes the order of events at crucial points, and he omits many vital incidents and sayings. For these and other reasons which we will discuss later, John's Gospel is usually studied apart from the first three.

Matthew, Mark, and Luke, by contrast, are so similar in vocabulary, content, and order of events that they are often printed in parallel columns and carefully compared with one another. Such an investigation reveals that they often agree not only in ideas but in punctuation, word order, and sentence structure. Because of their striking similarities and common point of view they are often called the Synoptic Gospels, from a Greek word meaning "looked at together." *The Gospel Parallels* (Thomas Nelson & Sons, 1957), an edition of the first three Gospels printed in parallel columns, is an invaluable tool for all serious students of the life of Jesus.

The so-called "Synoptic problem," one of the standard problems of New Testament study, is the attempt to construct a theory that will account for the similarities and differences of the first three Gospels by determining their relationship, sources, and chronological order. At first, scholars believed that all three Synoptic authors had copied from a common oral or written source. Then it became obvious that Mark was the first Gospel written and that the other two had used it as a guide in the composition of their own work. Along with Mark, they had a collection of the sayings of Jesus (commonly called "Q") as well as an independent source or sources. A famous British scholar, B. H. Streeter, is responsible for the four-document hypothesis that makes use of this data to solve the Synoptic problem.

According to this hypothesis, Mark was written first. Matthew is made up of Mark plus Q plus his own source or sources, M. Luke is made up of Mark plus Q plus his own source or sources, L. In this way we can account for the similarities and differences of the first three Gospels. This is called the four-document hypothesis because it is based on four primary documents, Mark, Q, M, and L.

Of great significance for modern New Testament study is the work of the form critics, those who try to discover the form of the tradition concerning Jesus as it existed during the period of oral transmission. It is now certain that the composition of the traditions about Jesus actually took many years, beginning in the form of oral accounts handed down by those who heard Jesus and knew him. Very early many of these accounts were written in fragmentary form without any attempt to keep them in order. Finally, as we have seen, they were brought together into coherent Gospel narratives. Form criticism, from the German word *Formgeschichte,* attempts to get back of our present written Gospels to discover the forms in which the stories and sayings were handed down. Vigorous research now taking place in this field is forcing us to reshape many of our former conclusions. We are not as positive about the historicity of certain events, for example, nor are we sure that the Q hypothesis best accounts for the relationship between Matthew and Luke. Stimulated by the discovery of the Dead Sea scrolls, New Testament research has become more exciting than man's search for knowledge about atoms and outer space!

In addition to the general problem of the relationship of the Gospels, there is one specific issue that every interpreter of Mark finds most perplexing. What happened to the ending of this Gospel? The ending of our present version (Mark 16:9–20) is found in no early manuscript. Even in later manuscripts, these verses appear in several different forms, leading us to believe that they were added by an editor to round out a very rough and incomplete ending. Without this later addition the Gospel ends right in the middle of the resurrection story: "And they went out and fled from the tomb; for trembling and astonishment had come upon them; and they said nothing to any one, for they were afraid." In Greek the ending is even more abrupt, for the final word is one like our "however," never used at the end of a sentence. In addition, the author had indicated that he would tell of a meeting between the disciples and the risen Christ (Mark 14:28;16:7), but the Gospel breaks off before he arrives at this important event.

Many solutions to the problem have been suggested, but the most reasonable is that the last sheet of the Gospel was lost very early in its history. This would be the sheet on the outside of the roll, the one most easily damaged or subject to accidental loss. We have no idea how or when such damage occurred, but the theory of accident seems to be the most probable solution to a baffling problem. One prominent scholar has called the breaking off of Mark in the middle of a cardinal passage "perhaps the worst disaster that has befallen the New Testament."

3. Outline

1. Preparation (ch. 1:1–13)
2. Jesus in Galilee (chs. 1:14 to 9:50)
   a. About the Sea of Galilee (chs. 1:14 to 5:43)
   b. Wider travels (chs. 6:1 to 9:50)
3. Journey to Jerusalem (ch. 10:1–52)
4. Jesus in Jerusalem (chs. 11:1 to 15:47)
   a. Jerusalem ministry (chs. 11:1 to 12:44)
   b. Apocalyptic discourse (ch. 13:1–37)
   c. Passion narrative (chs. 14:1 to 15:47)
5. The empty tomb (ch. 16:1–8)

Chapter 15

The Gospel of Matthew

1. Background

MATTHEW'S GOSPEL is usually ranked "first among equals." Its unique value was recognized by those who placed it first in the canon, and it has maintained a lofty position in the life of the church ever since. Forty years after it was written it was quoted at Antioch as "the Gospel." By the end of the second century, Christian writers were quoting it more frequently than any other New Testament document. It has been called "the authoritative account of the life of Christ" and "the fundamental document of the Christian religion." Renan, the famous French scholar, spoke of Matthew as "the most important book in the world."

This position of eminence is due to many factors, but three stand out in particular: (*a*) Early tradition attributed the book to the apostle Matthew, thus giving it high prestige as the work of an eyewitness who had been close to Jesus throughout his ministry. (*b*) In both form and content it has proved an unusually effective manual of instruction for use in the life of the church, the kind of book, for example, that could be placed in the hands of new converts. (*c*) Its catholic or universal spirit commended it from the beginning as a source of authority for the growing church that had to include persons of widely divergent opinions and backgrounds. An investigation of these factors reveals why Matthew has been called the "representative Gospel."

Looking first at the problem of authorship, we find it necessary to raise some questions about the tradition of apostolic origin. Very few modern scholars believe it was written in its present form by "one of the Twelve." For one thing, it is a Greek Gospel based on Greek sources and obviously written for a predominantly Gentile church, probably in Syria. The Gospel itself gives no hint of Matthew's authorship. On the contrary, it depends heavily on Mark, a fact that hardly commends it as an eyewitness account. A careful reading usually confirms the opinion that it was not written by an eyewitness, but by one who skillfully brought together many traditions that he had received from the past. We also find it difficult to believe that Matthew lived long enough to write a book that reflects so much highly developed church life, such as we find toward the end of the first century.

The same Bishop Papias whom we quoted in reference to Mark also made a relevant comment about Matthew. Unfortunately, most of the book by Papias has been lost, but one important fragment reads: "Matthew composed the oracles [sayings] in the Hebrew language, but everyone interpreted them as he was able." If this is true, it is quite possible that the apostle's work became the core of the later Gospel that was then titled "according to Matthew" because of the earlier work he had done. We may then follow tradition in relating this work in some general way to the apostle, but we must admit that the author of the finished work is unknown. That he was a Jewish Christian seems quite likely, but we know little else about him.

The date of the Gospel cannot be set with precision, but there are many indications that it was written late in the first century. Since it depends heavily upon Mark, it must have been composed after that earlier Gospel was readily available. The author uses the phrase "to this day," which implies a considerable time after the events that he is describing. He alludes to persecutions and to the disappointment that was felt toward the end of the century at the delay in the expected return of the Lord. For these reasons we suggest a date near A.D. 80–90.

The author's main *purpose* in writing was to meet the needs of the church by furnishing an account of the life and teaching of Jesus that could be used as an authoritative manual of instruction and guidance. The Gospel's comprehensiveness, its form, and its ecclesiastical interests all lend themselves to the fulfillment of this purpose, leading us to believe that the writer had the church in mind at every stage of his work.

Matthew is, in every respect, the most comprehensive Gospel. It contains nearly all the narrative material of Mark, plus infancy and resurrection records and the fullest collection of Jesus' teaching (three fifths of this Gospel is devoted to teaching). Every phase of Jesus' ministry is emphasized and all the aspects of his teaching. Not only does the Evangelist preserve many sayings that do not appear elsewhere, he also groups them with remarkable skill. He has taken a short sermon of Jesus', for example, which is preserved in one chapter of Luke (ch. 6) and has filled it out with many other sayings to make the Sermon on the Mount (Matt., chs. 5 to 7), which countless persons accept as the classic description of the Christian life.

The form of this Gospel also suited it admirably for use in the churches as a manual of instruction. The other Gospels mingle the teaching and the record of Jesus' ministry, but Matthew has carefully arranged his material into sections that lend themselves well to public reading and individual study. He has kept the narrative and the teaching separate, alternating a section of Mark with a large block of material from the collected sayings of Jesus (Q). The arrangement of the teaching of Jesus into five long discourses, each with a general theme, is one of the unique features of this Gospel. These discourses may be outlined as follows: Sermon on the Mount (Matt., chs. 5 to 7); instructions to disciples (Matt., ch. 10); parables of the Kingdom (Matt. 13:1–52); community problems (Matt., ch. 18); and the future (Matt., chs. 23 to 25). Five times in the course of the Gospel the author uses the same phrase to mark the plan of his book: "And when Jesus had finished these sayings." We can readily see how helpful this arrangement would be for a new convert to Christianity or for church members seeking guidance on some difficult phase of the Christian life.

From a literary point of view, Matthew's Gospel falls somewhere between Mark's rugged style and Luke's literary artistry. It is written in clear, direct, and dignified language that is easily memorized or read in public. The author continually improves on Mark's rough form, changing the tense of verbs, substituting words, and generally avoiding repetition. He gives a great deal of attention to the matter of style, not for the sake of style in itself, but for the purpose of exalting the One about whom he was writing. Matthew's language nearly always advances his story and seldom gets in the way.

The author's obvious interest in the life of the church has led some interpreters to label Matthew as "the ecclesiastical Gospel." He is the only Evangelist who explicitly mentions the church (Matt. 16:18; 18:17). He refers some of the parables of Jesus to specific needs of the church, at times confusing the Kingdom that Jesus proclaimed with the visible church on earth. Elsewhere he tries to provide a church law to take the place of the old law of Moses, as in his directions on almsgiving, prayer, and fasting (Matt. 6:1-18), marriage and divorce (Matt. 5:27-32), and the relation of Christians to children and fellow believers (Matt. 18:10-14; 7:12; 18:15-22).

His ecclesiastical concern is also reflected in his great interest in Simon Peter, who became such a prominent leader in the life of the early church. Only Matthew includes the important promises of Jesus, "You are Peter, and on this rock I will build my church," and "I will give you the keys of the kingdom of heaven" (Matt. 16:18-19). This Gospel is also the only one that tells of Peter's attempt to walk on the water and of his concern about paying the Temple tax for Jesus and himself. We thus have two Gospels closely related to Peter: Mark, which is based upon Peter's memories of Jesus, and Matthew, which is interested in Peter because of his position of leadership in the life of the church.

Finally, in assessing the great popularity of this Gospel, we must stress the value of its catholic or universal outlook. The Evangelist has been accused of inconsistency at some points, but this is only because of his eagerness to set forth many different phases of Christian opinion. Convinced that the one church could include persons of divergent viewpoints, he wrote in a tolerant spirit, trying to include as many representative views as possible. This was a leading factor in winning for Matthew the first position in the canon of the New Testament.

This attempt to express varying points of view is vividly illustrated by his portrait of Jesus as the fulfillment of Jewish prophecy and the universal Savior of mankind.

Nearly every chapter includes some prophetic passage that is related to the general formula, "All this took place to fulfill what the Lord had spoken by the prophet." In all, he refers to the Old Testament well over a hundred times in quotations or allusions, trying to show how Jesus fulfilled the hopes of Judaism. He revises Mark's Gospel at times to make it conform to prophetic statements, even to the extent of having Jesus ride two donkeys into Jerusalem in order to fulfill the letter of the prophecy (Matt. 21:7). Other Jewish tendencies of this writer are seen in his emphasis on the law, including the practice of almsgiving, prayer, and fasting, and in his avoidance of the sacred name for God. This is the Gospel which substitutes "Kingdom of Heaven" for "Kingdom of God."

Alongside this Jewish tendency, however, we must place the author's stress on the universal mission of Jesus as the world's Savior. His disciples are instructed to show love to all men without distinction (Matt. 5:43 f.) and they are sent out to "make disciples of all nations" (Matt. 28:19). When the Kingdom comes, many will be gathered into it from the east and the west, while "the sons of the kingdom will be thrown into the outer darkness" (Matt. 8:11–12). The Pharisees are condemned with fierce woes, and a Gentile centurion is warmly praised. According to the parable of the Last Judgment, "all nations" will be gathered to obtain reward or punishment for their deeds (Matt. 25:32 f.).

We thus find in the same Gospel a narrow Jewish concept of Jesus as Messiah and a broad universal approach to Christ as Savior. This is not an inconsistency, but a conviction on the author's part that there is a place in the life of the church for all sincere opinions about Christ. As we have seen, Paul wrote at a time when certain points of view were in danger of annihilation. Toward the end of the century, however, many of the old animosities had subsided and the divergent factions were drawing closer together. Matthew's Gospel became the foundation for an ideal church that was beyond factional divisions, and strong enough to include many points of view. This fact, better than any other, explains why Matthew writes so meaningfully about the Messiah who is also the Savior of the world.

2. *Problems*

The chief textual problems involved in any study of the Gospels include the attempt to discover and relate the sources that the authors have used in the composition of their finished work. A majority of scholars agree, for example, that Matthew used the Gospel of Mark as the basis for his own book. We can find at least fifteen sixteenths of Mark reproduced in Matthew, and the part that is missing does not appear in any significant blocks of material, but in small bits and fragments. For the most part, Matthew reproduces the order and arrangement of Mark's phrases to an extraordinary degree. His heavy dependence upon his Marcan source has led some to call Matthew "a revised and enlarged Gospel of Mark." This is an exaggeration for purposes of emphasis, but it does highlight the close relationship between the first two Gospels.

One of the most intriguing problems of New Testament study arises in the search for sources outside of Mark that the other Gospels have used. Unlike Mark, these other sources were not preserved after being incorporated into the longer Gospels, but anyone reading the introduction to Luke's Gospel cannot doubt that many such sources existed. One of them, commonly called Q (from the German word *Quelle*, "source"), is now a generally accepted principle in New Testament interpretation. There have been

some attempts among modern scholars to discredit the Q
theory, but their conclusions have not been widely ac-
cepted.

The Q document is uncovered when we deduct from
Matthew and Luke that portion of their contents which is
derived from Mark. In doing so, we discover approxi-
mately two hundred verses which they have in common,
nearly all of which are concerned with the teaching or
words of Jesus. It is reasonable to assume that the authors
of Matthew and Luke had a collection of Jesus' sayings
that they used, along with Mark, as a common source. As
a matter of fact, the longer Gospels may have been written
to bring the story of Jesus' life and the collection of his
sayings together, "the things which Jesus said and did."

The Q source was undoubtedly one of the earliest de-
posits of Gospel tradition. It is unlikely that it was ever a
fixed document like Mark, but was fluid and changing,
passing through a number of versions. Each Christian com-
munity may have possessed its own copy of Q, which it
would revise as new sayings became available. The writers
of Matthew and Luke probably had two different versions
of Q, evidence of which may be seen in the two different
versions of the Beatitudes and the Lord's Prayer (Matt.
5:3–12 and Luke 6:20–23; Matt. 6:9–15 and Luke 11:2–4).
Although Q existed in many versions, however, it never-
theless retained its general character as a "manual of the
Lord's teaching." To this extent we may refer to it as a
definite source, supremely valuable because of its early
origin.

What other sources did the author of this Gospel use?
About a quarter of his material does not appear in Mark
or Q, thus leading us to suppose that he used several
sources of his own. His version of the Christmas story
(Matt. 1:18–23) and several parables (e.g., Matt., ch. 25)

illustrate this use of independent sources.

The search for these various oral and written traditions must be left to the New Testament specialists whose task has become increasingly challenging in recent years. We certainly cannot agree with the German scholar who described source analysis of the Synoptic gospels as "scavenger's labors in which one is choked with dust." Advanced research sometimes raises a frightful cloud of dust, but when the dust settles we often find ourselves on firm ground with a view of wider horizons. The ever-increasing use of source analysis is proving its value in taking us closer to the primitive traditions about the life and words of Jesus.

3. Outline

1. The Nativity (chs. 1 and 2)
2. The life and teaching of Jesus (chs. 3 to 25)
   a. Part One: (chs. 3 to 7)
      (1) Narrative: baptism and temptation (chs. 3 and 4)
      (2) First discourse: Sermon on the Mount (chs. 5 to 7)
   b. Part Two: (chs. 8 to 10)
      (1) Narrative: nine miracles (chs. 8 and 9)
      (2) Second discourse: instructions to disciples (ch. 10)
   c. Part Three: (chs. 11:1 to 13:52)
      (1) Narrative: questions and controversies (chs. 11 and 12)
      (2) Third discourse: parables of the Kingdom (ch. 13:1–52)
   d. Part Four: (chs. 13:53 to 18:35)
      (1) Narrative: miracles and teaching for disciples (chs. 13:53 to 17:27)

Chapter 16

The Gospel of Luke

1. Background

A N UNFORTUNATE divorce occurred in the second century when Luke and The Acts were separated and placed apart from one another in the New Testament canon. They belong together (Luke-Acts), for they were written by the same author as two volumes of a single work.

The preface to the Gospel is the preface to the whole, as we see in the brief reference at the beginning of The Acts. Separating them obscures their essential unity and violates the author's intention to present to the world a comprehensive history of the rise and spread of the Christian religion.

Luke and The Acts, taken as two volumes of a single work, represent a little more than one fourth of the New Testament, the largest block of material by a single writer. On the basis of quantity alone they deserve all of the care that has been lavished upon them by generations of scholars. But there is much more than quantity involved. The author was the first Christian historian, giving us not only a full "biography" of Jesus, but also our most valuable record of the life of the early church. He wrote in a matchless style, Renan calling his Gospel "the most beautiful book ever written." The entire work is characterized by joy and gladness at the good news of God's mighty act that is intended for the salvation of the entire world.

From earliest times the author of the two-volume work has been recognized as Luke, Paul's companion, who was also known as "the beloved physician" (Col. 4:14). Apparently subject to some form of chronic illness, Paul would welcome the company of a physician on his many journeys. Such an arrangement undoubtedly gave Luke the opportunity to gather much of the information used in his two-volume history. In describing the history of the church he occasionally slips into the use of the first person plural, indicating that he was an eyewitness and participant in many of the events that he describes ("We sought to go on into Macedonia"). The church has always regarded Luke as the author of both books, and we see no reason to doubt this judgment.

As far as we can determine, both volumes of Luke's work appeared about the same time. The Gospel depends heavily upon Mark (ca. A.D. 70), yet knows nothing about Paul's letters, even contradicting them at points. These letters were in general circulation by the end of the first century, and any Pauline biographer would have used them as his chief source of information. Luke, therefore, must have written before these letters were commonly known. For these and other reasons, the date of Luke-Acts is usually set about A.D. 90–95. Luke must always be remembered as the first Christian historian. His central *purpose* is to bring together the miscellaneous records about Jesus and the church into one coherent historical account. No other work in the New Testament opens with such a formal preface stating the author's intention:

Inasmuch as many have undertaken to compile a narrative of the things which have been accomplished among us,

just as they were delivered to us by those who from the
beginning were eyewitnesses and ministers of the word, it
seemed good to me also, having followed all things closely
for some time past, to write an orderly account for you,
most excellent Theophilus, that you may know the truth
concerning the things of which you have been informed.
(Luke 1:1–4.)

Four of the most important criteria of sound scholarship
have been included in this statement: inclusiveness, ac-
curacy, proper order, and the use of primary sources. His
inclusiveness is especially noteworthy. In the case of the
Gospel he is anxious to provide an adequate biography of
Jesus that will lead into his second-volume description of
the spread of Christianity from Jerusalem to Rome. In the
Gospel he begins with the birth of John the Baptist and
includes far more of the Nativity story than any other
writer. He is the only one who includes any event from
Jesus' boyhood (Luke 2:41–52). At another crucial point
he sets aside Mark's order and includes a long section
(Luke 9:51 to 18:14) that describes events and the teach-
ings of Jesus during the journey to Jerusalem. He makes
a great effort to date events with accuracy: "In those days
a decree went out from Caesar Augustus that all the world
should be enrolled. This was the first enrollment, when
Quirinius was governor of Syria" (Luke 2:1–2). In these
and many other ways, Luke proves himself a capable his-
torian, providing us with an invaluable record of early
Christianity.

It is quite obvious, however, that Luke's historical moti-
vation was not the only purpose for writing. For one thing,
he was anxious to answer charges of sedition by proving
that Jesus was not a political revolutionary intent on over-
turning the Roman government. Persecutions arose as soon
as it became clear that Christianity was not simply a Jew-

ish sect but a separate movement whose founder had been duly examined and condemned by a Roman court. This was sufficient proof that he was politically dangerous, for Roman justice could not be challenged. In the Gospels of Mark and Matthew there is an obvious attempt on the part of Christian apologists to show that the Jews, and the Jews only, were responsible for the execution of Jesus. His death was strictly a religious matter and had nothing to do with politics. Luke carries this apologetic interest farther, going out of his way to stress the moral and religious nature of Jesus' ministry and teaching. In Luke's account of the trial of Jesus, Pilate asserts no less than three times that he found no evidence for a criminal charge. Herod Antipas agreed. The blame is laid entirely on the Jews in contrast to the Romans, whose view is represented by the centurion at the foot of the cross: "Certainly this man was innocent!" Luke's defense of Christianity is developed still further in the book of The Acts where it is shown that Christians, like their founder, are interested in religious matters and not in politics.

Another of Luke's primary interests is the desire to show how Christ came as the Savior of the entire world. Luke, the only Gentile among the Gospel writers, composed a universal Gospel. Jesus, according to Luke, had been born under the Jewish law, but he had transcended it. His ancestry should be traced back to Adam, the primal man, rather than to Abraham, the father of the Jewish people. We are shown how Jesus recognized faith in publicans, and made Samaritans the heroes of many of his stories. In Luke's Gospel there is no suggestion that Jesus wanted to limit the gospel to certain groups (cf. Matt. 10:5; 15:24), and Mark's story of the pagan woman whose request was grudgingly fulfilled is omitted (Mark 7:24–30). Thus Luke prepares the way for the story in The Acts of the spread of this universal religion throughout the pagan world.

It has also been suggested that Luke had a missionary motive in preparing his two-volume work. He was writing for Christians, but he also wanted to attract the Gentile public to Christ. This is apparent from the general character of his work, which is written in better Greek than are any of the other Gospels. He carefully fashioned his story so that it would appeal to people who knew nothing about Jesus or who might be prejudiced against him. He wanted those who started the story to become involved and follow it to the end. This is one reason why he chose his words carefully, balanced his sentences, and constantly improved on Mark's rugged style. Many passages in his Gospel stand alone as literary masterpieces. The parable of the good Samaritan, the story of Mary and Martha, the parable of the prodigal son, and the account of the walk to Emmaus are written in such matchless literary style that one fourth-century scholar concluded that Luke must have been an artist. While enjoying his style, however, we must not forget that it was intended to serve a missionary purpose, commending Christ and his message to the Gentile world. This purpose is clearly seen in the fact that Luke's style, like Matthew's, never calls attention to itself, but always to its subject, Christ the Savior of the world.

In telling his story of Jesus, Luke includes certain characteristics that give his Gospel a unique quality. He emphasizes the *prayer* life of Jesus, recording more words of Jesus about prayer and more reports of Jesus praying than any other writer. His Gospel betrays a marked interest in the role of *women* in the gospel tradition. Many more women appear in his record than in any other, and Jesus seems to treat them with special tenderness and concern. He also shows unusual sympathy for the *poor*. The Magnificat's declaration that God has "filled the hungry with good things, and the rich he has sent empty away" becomes a kind of theme for the entire gospel. Finally, Luke is particularly interested in the *parables* of Jesus, including in his record many that do not appear in the other Gospels, among them the matchless stories of the good Samaritan and the prodigal son. All these characteristics help to make Luke's portrait of Jesus one of the most memorable ever created.

2. Problems

The main problem facing the interpreter of this Gospel is the large amount of material that cannot be attributed to Mark or Q. About two fifths of Luke may be assigned to Mark, and about one fifth to Q. This leaves two fifths that must be traced to other sources. The two outstanding examples of Luke's use of independent traditions are the infancy narratives (Luke, chs. 1 and 2) and the so-called "long insertion" (Luke 9:51 to 18:14) where he abandons Mark and introduces a great mass of his own material. This insertion is sometimes called the "travel document" because it supposedly describes incidents that occurred on the journey to Jerusalem.

We know very little about the origin of Luke's special sources. It is customary to speak of the L document, but this may be misleading, since Luke tells us that he used many sources. The infancy narratives, for example, are strikingly different from the rest of the Gospel and may have come from the early Palestinian church. About the best we can say is that Luke used Mark and Q in the composition of his Gospel, adding to them a great deal of material from other sources, one of which may have been substantial enough to deserve the designation "L" or "Luke's special source." Modern research may clarify the picture, but Luke was so skillful in blending his material that any source analysis is extremely difficult.

Another theory about Luke's Gospel should be considered briefly. Impressed by Luke's special section and his omission of much Marcan material, some scholars believe that he wrote a first edition of his Gospel before Mark became available to him. This first edition, called Proto-Luke, was compiled from his own sources and Q. Later, when he found Mark, he inserted it into his earlier work and produced our present Gospel. This theory explains some of the difficulties in Luke, but it has not won general acceptance. Fortunately, our appreciation of the four Gospels does not depend upon our ability to reconstruct their sources, but in Luke's case it would be very helpful, because he tells us that much of his information came to him from those who were "eyewitnesses and ministers of the word."

3. Outline

1. Preface (ch. 1:1–4)
2. Preparation (chs. 1:5 to 4:13)
3. Ministry in Galilee (chs. 4:14 to 9:50)
   a. Nazareth and Capernaum (chs. 4:14 to 6:11)
   b. The Twelve (ch. 6:12–49)
   c. Miracles and teaching (chs. 7:1 to 9:27)
   d. Transfiguration (ch. 9:28–50)
4. Journey to Jerusalem (chs. 9:51 to 19:27)
   a. Various teachings (chs. 9:51 to 18:30)
   b. Prediction of the Passion (ch. 18:31–34)
   c. In Jericho (chs. 18:35 to 19:27)
5. Ministry in Jerusalem (chs. 19:28 to 21:38)
   a. Entry and Temple-cleansing (chs. 19:28 to 19:46)
   b. Opposition from many groups (chs. 19:47 to 20:47)
   c. "The Little Apocalypse" (ch. 21)
6. Passion and death (chs. 22 and 23)
7. Resurrection (ch. 24)

Chapter 17

The Acts of the Apostles

1. Background

THE SECOND volume of Luke's comprehensive work on the birth and growth of Christianity is usually called The Acts of the Apostles. The title is misleading, however, for the book is mainly concerned with Peter and Paul and with only a few of their activities. A more accurate title might be "Some Acts of Some Apostles," but this does not indicate that the real theme of the book is the expansion of Christianity from Jerusalem to Rome. It might be helpful to know what the author called his own work, but the original title was lost when Luke and The Acts were separated. His plan is clear, however, for he uses incidents from the lives of Peter, Paul, and two or three others to tell the exciting story of how Christianity, which began in such an insignificant way, spread in ever-widening circles until it reached Rome, the center of the world.

It would be difficult to overestimate the historical value of The Acts. No comparable narrative covering the origin and development of the Christian movement has survived. Luke's Gospel is one of the richest of the Synoptics, and its loss would be tragic, but we do have other Gospels that cover much of the same ground. The loss of The Acts would be a very different story, because we do not have any other source of information for most of the events it describes. Paul's letters are helpful, but many of his references would be hopelessly obscure apart from the record available in Luke's volume. The Acts is unique and invaluable because it is the only bridge across the gulf that separates "Jesus from Paul, Christ from Christianity, the gospel of Jesus from the gospel about Jesus."

In the previous chapter we suggested that Luke-Acts was written by Luke, the beloved physician, late in the first century, perhaps about A.D. 90. The most serious challenge to this generally accepted hypothesis comes from those who are deeply troubled by the abrupt ending of The Acts. After telling so much about Paul, the book suddenly ends with the apostle in his Roman prison, awaiting trial. A great deal of interest in the book centers around the fortunes of Paul after he has made his appeal to Caesar, but we never discover how the story ends. Some interpreters insist that the book must have been written about A.D. 64 while Luke was awaiting the outcome of the trial. If he had known the result, he certainly would have reported it. Against this argument it must be emphasized (a) that Luke-Acts was written after Mark (ca. A.D. 70), (b) that Paul's death seems to be implied in the book (e.g., Acts 20:38), and (c) that Luke's intention was not to write a complete biography of Paul but to describe the expansion of the faith to Rome. His book is therefore rounded out and concluded as far as his main purpose is concerned. Many other suggestions have been made to account for the abrupt ending of the book (Luke intended a third volume; Paul was condemned by the Romans), but whatever the answer, the fact cannot be used to prove a date as early as A.D. 64.

Luke's historical *purpose* pervades both volumes of his work. His desire is to compile an accurate record of Jesus and the early church from his many sources, but in the book of The Acts we can see a vital religious motive taking shape behind the historical narrative. By demonstrating how the movement that began obscurely in Galilee had spread to the world's capital, Luke is trying to use Christianity's success as the best evidence of its truth and validity. The apostles were ordinary men, but they had achieved extraordinary results. They had overcome insurmountable difficulties because the power of God was with them. In view of the amazing success of Christianity, who could doubt that Jesus was truly the Son of God?

This religious-historical motive accounts for the over-all plan of The Acts in which Luke devotes most of his attention to Peter (one third of his book) and Paul (one half of his book). His real interest is not in the activities of the apostles, but in the way in which events in the lives of the two chief apostles illustrate the expansion of the faith. The volume is divided into six distinct sections, each ending with a formula indicating that the next is about to begin. Beginning with the origin of the church in Jerusalem, Luke shows how the movement spread through Palestine, Syria, Asia Minor, and Europe, finally ending in Rome, the world's capital. These ever-widening circles of influence provide the framework for the unfolding story, which is told with dramatic effect.

Luke's desire to validate Christianity by emphasizing its success accounts for some of his defects as a historian. It has been pointed out that his "incomplete record" omits considerable information on matters of utmost importance. Even Paul's career is sketched in a fragmentary way. Luke's carelessness in matters of detail has also caused concern. The three accounts of Paul's conversion, for example, all agree on the main facts, but vary hopelessly in details (Acts, chs. 9;22;26). These "defects" clearly show that Luke's purpose was not to report history as such, but to use history in proving the validity of Christianity.

Another of the author's purposes in The Acts, as in the Gospel, is to defend Christianity against charges of sedition. In the first "volume" of his work, Luke tries to prove that Jesus was not a political revolutionary condemned by Roman courts but a religious teacher murdered by the Jews. In his second volume, he shows even more explicitly that the church is in no way opposed to the Roman government. Paul's Roman citizenship is stressed, along with the fact that he was often protected by Roman officials. Luke pointedly reports the number of Romans who became converts and places all the blame for opposition to Christianity on the malice of the Jews. It has been suggested that the preface implies an apologetic interest when it expresses a desire to have Theophilus, a Roman official, "know the truth" about Christianity.

Other themes from the Gospel, such as the universalism of Christianity, are also developed in The Acts, confirming our belief that the two volumes were composed as a unit. In addition, there is one important new dimension that is developed throughout the book of The Acts. For the first time we are introduced to the life of the early church and made to feel its strength and vigor. Early in The Acts, Luke describes with intense dramatic power the birth of the church on the Day of Pentecost. Ever since that moment, he insists, the community of believers has been led and guided by the Holy Spirit, a fact that proves that the church is an integral part of the Christ-event initiated by God. Modern Christians, deeply concerned about the present lack of spiritual vitality in many phases of church life, are asking, What was the secret of spiritual strength in the

early church? At least three possible answers are suggested
by Luke's record in The Acts: (*a*) a vivid awareness of the
Holy Spirit; (*b*) a burning conviction of the saving power
of Jesus Christ; (*c*) a deep sense of Christ-centered fellow-
ship (*koinōnia*).

The Holy Spirit is one of the most prominent concepts
in Luke's work. There are only eighteen references to the
Spirit in Matthew and Mark combined, but Luke uses the
term nearly sixty times in the book of The Acts alone. The
church came into being when the Holy Spirit came from
heaven like a mighty wind and fire. The Spirit was "poured
out" on some disciples, while others were "filled with" it.
The Spirit instructed Peter, "caught up" Philip, told Paul
and Timothy not to speak the word in certain places, and
guided the selection of apostles. This vivid awareness of
the Spirit, the living presence of God, helps to explain the
sense of joy, power, and vitality so evident in the primitive
church described by Luke.

The members of the church also had a burning convic-
tion of the saving power of Jesus Christ. Their own lives
had been transformed because of the new relationship to
God that his life, teaching, death, and resurrection had
made possible. Through the Christ-event they had been
transformed into "new creatures" and they could not stop
telling others about this good thing which had happened to
them. The theme of all their sermons was this saving power
of Christ. Whenever they ate together in a common meal,
they "remembered" Jesus who had brought them into this
new life. Freed by Christ, from the legalism of Judaism
and the emptiness of paganism, they could not stop talking
about this act of God which made all things new.

Finally, they found themselves living in a new kind of
fellowship with one another. Because our English word
"fellowship" has been so diluted, it is highly desirable to

use the Greek word *koinōnia* to describe the kind of life-sharing into which these Christians entered. They found themselves concerned about one another with a selfless, compassionate love they had never known before. Paul describes it in one of his letters when he says the whole fellowship rejoiced when one member felt joy and suffered when one member felt pain. A pagan observer remarked in amazement, "See how these Christians love one another!" They lived together, prayed together, worked together, and even tried to share all of their possessions for a time. There is a world of meaning in Luke's simple description of the new life of the converts who came into the church on the Day of Pentecost: "And they devoted themselves to the apostles' teaching and fellowship [*koinōnia*], to the breaking of bread and the prayers" (Acts 2:42). Perhaps those seeking new spiritual life for the modern church will find it in these elements which gave life to the church in the beginning.

2. Problems

As in the case of the Gospel, Luke has used many sources in compiling his second volume. Unfortunately, all these documents have disappeared, so that it is practically impossible to trace them with any accuracy or certainty. Along with written documents, the Evangelist undoubtedly used much oral information that he had gathered while traveling with Paul. It has been suggested that his chief authority for some episodes was Philip, whereas for others he turned to Mary, the mother of Jesus. All of this is pure conjecture, but it certainly is not difficult to imagine a man of Luke's far-ranging interests searching eagerly for information at every opportunity.

The only source that can be identified and isolated to some extent contained the so-called "we" sections. Suddenly and quite unexpectedly, Luke breaks into the use of the first person plural in four sections of The Acts (Acts 16:10–17; 20:5–15; 21:1–18; 27:1 to 28:16). These "we" sections appear to be fragments from a diary or journal kept by a travel companion of Paul's. It is now generally believed that Luke used his own travel diary, at times skillfully blending it with his other sources. On occasion he demonstrates unusual sensitivity by retaining the original wording to gain an effect of firsthand participation. This use of his own vivid travel diary, along with the careful selection of dramatic events from his sources, makes Luke's second volume one of the most exciting books ever written.

3. Outline

1. Origin of the church at Jerusalem (chs. 1:1 to 6:7)
2. Extension of the church through Palestine (chs. 6:8 to 9:31)
3. Extension of the church to Syria (chs. 9:32 to 12:24)
4. Extension of the church through Asia Minor (chs. 12:25 to 16:5)
5. Extension of the church to Europe (chs. 16:6 to 19:20)
6. Extension of the church to Rome (chs. 19:21 to 28:31)

Chapter 18

First Peter

1. Background

THIS LETTER, often overlooked by the casual reader, is one of the most beautiful in the New Testament. Its spirit is lofty and noble, reflecting the deep religious experience of the writer and the purity of his life in Christ. When we remember the severity of the type of persecution that called it forth, the letter's undaunted courage and noble piety become even more meaningful, and we can understand why it is often called "the epistle of hope."

The fact that it was written against the background of bitter persecution is obvious on every page. Again and again the author refers to the suffering that has spread to the "brotherhood throughout the world." He speaks of suffering "various trials," of suffering "patiently," and of suffering "for righteousness' sake." He exhorts his readers to "be prepared to make a defense," and to keep a clear conscience in order to shame those who abuse them. "Beloved," he warns them, "do not be surprised at the fiery ordeal which comes upon you to prove you. . . . But rejoice in so far as you share Christ's sufferings. . . . If one suffers as a Christian, let him not be ashamed. . . . Therefore let those who suffer according to God's will do right and entrust their souls to a faithful creator." (I Peter 4:12–19.)

Attempts to identify the persecutions that are alluded to by the writer lead us to the difficult problem of authorship. Was the letter written by Simon Peter? It was addressed to Christians in Asia Minor (I Peter 1:1), but so far as we know there was no organized persecution in the provinces until late in the first century. Further evidence for a late date is found in the fact that the name "Christian" by itself was sufficient ground for condemnation (I Peter 4:14). For these reasons, most commentators date the letter about A.D. 96, during the cruel persecution by Domitian, the same crisis that gave rise to the book of The Revelation. If this date is true, however, then the letter cannot have been written by Peter, who died during the reign of Nero in A.D. 62 or 64. Further evidence that Peter did not write it may be listed as follows: (*a*) the letter demonstrates a command of the Greek language unlikely in a Galilean fisherman; (*b*) it is clearly indebted to Paul; (*c*) it does not sound like the work of one who had known Jesus intimately.

There seems little doubt, on the other hand, that the letter originated in Rome. "She who is at Babylon, who is likewise chosen, sends you greetings." (I Peter 5:13.) The same symbol is used in The Revelation to refer to the persecuting Empire (Rev. 17:5,9). Because of this Roman origin, it is easy to understand why the letter would be sent out under Peter's name. The church in Rome cherished the memory of Peter and felt that they could speak for him because of his close association with them. Their sense of identification with him was especially strong because they had witnessed his martyrdom. Add to this the fact that Paul's collected letters were reviving memories of his life and work and we can understand why the

Roman Christians wished to send out a letter in the name
of Peter. The writer and the Roman church do not expect
the Asian Christians to believe that the letter was actually
written by Peter, but they do want them to feel that it
comes with the "authority" of that great apostle.

Against this background the author's *purpose* be-
comes quite clear. He writes to persecuted Christians to
strengthen and encourage them by reminding them (*a*) of
the glory of their new life in Christ and (*b*) of the Chris-
tian hope that is a result of it.

Along with the other New Testament documents, this
letter abounds with references to the new life in Christ
that has come to the author and to his fellow Christians.
Reflecting the practice of the early preachers, he reminds
his readers of the way in which Christ's life, death, and
resurrection had opened for them a new way to God. "By
his great mercy we have been born anew to a living hope
through the resurrection of Jesus Christ from the dead,
and to an inheritance which is imperishable, undefiled,
and unfading." (I Peter 1:3–4.) Because of this new rela-
tionship to God, Christians have entered into a new rela-
tionship of love with their fellows. "Having purified your
souls, . . . love one another earnestly from the heart." (I
Peter 1:22.) Even the most casual reader can sense the
holy joy that this writer feels because of his new relation-
ship to God and to his brothers in Christ.

The main thing about this Christian life which the
author wishes to share with his persecuted brethren is un-
dying hope. Here is no superficial hope that things will
get better by-and-by, but a hope that is grounded in ab-
solute trust in the God who works through Jesus Christ to
achieve his eternal purpose among men. Persecutions come
and go, but those who hope in Christ bear them with cour-
age, knowing that all things are in the hands of God. Even

Christ underwent the extremity of suffering and bore it with patience and trust in the Father. (I Peter 2:21–24.) This mood is very different from that of The Revelation, which speaks of the persecutors in violent and bitter tones. We feel in this letter a great gentleness and patience under suffering, all made possible by the hope that arises out of complete submission to the will of God. It has been suggested with good cause that hope plays the same part in First Peter that faith does in the letters of Paul.

This great theme of hope is also developed by the author in terms of expectations about the future. Christians may have confidence not only because everything is in the hands of God but also because God will soon bring history to an end and judge all men. "The end of all things is at hand." (I Peter 4:7.) "For the time has come for judgment to begin with the household of God; and if it begins with us, what will be the end of those who do not obey the gospel of God?" (I Peter 4:17.) First Peter is not a thoroughgoing apocalyptic writing, but it does reflect much of the same excitement that we feel in Paul's letters to Thessalonica and in The Revelation. The suffering now is hard to endure, but mighty Babylon (Rome) will be destroyed by the power of God. "And after you have suffered a little while, the God of all grace, who has called you to his eternal glory in Christ, will himself restore, establish, and strengthen you. To him be the dominion for ever and ever. Amen." (I Peter 5:10–11.)

Before closing our discussion of the background of this letter, we should note one distinctive idea that has caused a great deal of perplexity among later Christians. According to this author, Christ descended to the world of the dead after his own crucifixion and preached the gospel to the disobedient of all ages in order that they might obtain new life. After the crucifixion, Christ was "made alive in the spirit; in which he went and preached to the spirits in prison, who formerly did not obey" (I Peter 3:18–20). The same idea is expressed in another way: "For this is why the gospel was preached even to the dead, that though judged in the flesh like men, they might live in the spirit like God" (I Peter 4:6).

Modern Christians are often confused by this strange belief when they confront it in the Apostles' Creed: "He descended into hell." We are not sure where this idea first arose. It may have grown out of speculation about the interval between Christ's death and resurrection or out of concern for the salvation of those who died before Christ came. The latter question has arisen in every generation, for if salvation is through Christ, What about those who lived before his coming? To answer this, the doctrine arose that Christ proclaimed the gospel among the dead. This idea did not originate in First Peter, but it is first stated here as an accepted article of Christian belief.

2. Problems

The theory of authorship suggested above is by no means unanimously accepted, some interpreters insisting quite firmly that Peter wrote this document. "An epistle truly worthy of the chief of the apostles," said John Calvin, "full of apostolic authority and majesty."

Supporters of this view point to the strong tradition of Petrine authorship that appeared very early and remained unchallenged for many centuries. They are not impressed with the argument that Peter could not write such excellent Greek, for Peter tells us that he wrote through a "secretary" (I Peter 5:12). Nor will they accept the arguments that the letter depends too much on Paul and exhibits too little knowledge of the life and teaching of Jesus. On the contrary, they insist that the general tone and temper of the epistle reflect the early days of the church and that it contains nothing that might not have come from the thought and experience of Peter. According to this view, the letter was written by Peter from Rome just before the persecutions of Nero that claimed Peter's life in A.D. 64.

We do not need to repeat the very convincing arguments that have been forwarded in opposition to this theory. It should be noted, however, that our failure to achieve absolute certainty on such matters does not detract from the religious value of this letter. It reminds Christians in every generation of their hope in Christ.

3. Outline

1. Salutation (ch. 1:1–2)
2. The blessings of Christians (chs. 1:3 to 2:10)
   a. The Christian hope (ch. 1:3–12)
   b. Moral obligations of this hope (chs. 1:13 to 2:10)
3. The duties of Christians (chs. 2:11 to 4:11)
   a. Various duties (chs. 2:11 to 4:6)
   b. The ethics of crisis (ch. 4:7–11)
4. The trials of Christians (chs. 4:12 to 5:11)
   a. Christians under persecution (ch. 4:12–19)
   b. Concluding exhortation (ch. 5:1–11)
5. Conclusion (ch. 5:12–14)

Chapter 19

The Revelation to John

1. Background

THE FIRST century was a dangerous age for Christians! Jesus had been crucified because of his teaching, and many apostles, including Peter and Paul, had met death because of loyalty to him. Members of the church in Rome and in every province were in constant danger from the violence of mobs and the organized persecution of Roman rulers. Under such circumstances we should not be surprised to find a variety of reactions on the part of the Christians. Many weak church members denied Christ in order to save their lives. Others compromised, going through the forms of emperor worship without believing what they were doing. Some faced the crisis with quiet courage and deep faith, as we have just seen in First Peter. A few, however, raised bitter voices of defiance and rejoiced at the punishment that the righteous God was about to inflict on the harlot Roman Empire. This was the spirit of the book of The Revelation.

When it was written, its purpose was easily understood by its readers. It was directed to their immediate situation and was related to their immediate needs. They well un-

derstood its strange cryptic language because they were
familiar with many other books written in the same way.
But after the immediate crisis had passed and the type of
language was forgotten, the book became a storm center
of controversy. From the middle of the second century it
has been a much disputed, mysterious work. The mystery
and disputation have increased with the passing of time, so
that many modern Christians feel hopelessly lost as they
approach The Revelation. This should not be, for in many
ways it is the simplest of all New Testament writings. In
order to understand it, however, two facts must be kept
constantly in mind: (*a*) The Revelation was written to
meet the immediate needs of a specific first-century situa-
tion; (*b*) it was written in an apocalyptic form very famil-
iar to its first readers.

One of the strangest errors in the interpretation of The
Revelation has been the assumption that its contents refer
to some distant future. As a result, endless attempts have
been made to apply its prophecies to events in later his-
tory, including the twentieth century! Every year there are
newspaper accounts of some poor soul who sells every-
thing, wraps himself in a sheet, and goes up on a mountain
to wait for the end of the world because he has found a
prediction in the book of The Revelation. Every war has
been called the battle of Armageddon and every dictator
the Antichrist. After two thousand years we might have
learned our lesson, but, alas, fanciful speculation continues
unabated.

The author himself plainly tells us that he is writing
for his own time. "The revelation of Jesus Christ, which
God gave him to show to his servants what must soon take
place; . . . the time is near." (Rev. 1:1,3.) This note is
struck in the opening words and continues until the end:
"Do not seal up the words of the prophecy of this book,

for the time is near. . . . Behold, I am coming soon" (Rev. 22:10,12). It is obvious from these words and from the whole mood of the book that the author expected all that was predicted in it to take place almost immediately.

The crisis that called it forth was the bitter persecution under Emperor Domitian about A.D. 95–96. Prior to his reign, most of the rulers had permitted emperor worship but they had not encouraged it. Domitian, on the other hand, for personal and political reasons, pressed the issue so far that Christians had to choose between death and worship of the emperor as a god. Domitian required public sacrifices to himself and ordered his household to call him "our Lord and God." He called his bed the couch of a god and referred to his food as sacred. His demands were enforced with such ruthless zeal that he was finally assassinated by one of his vengeful servants.

One of those who refused to observe the official cult was a man named John, a leader in the churches of Asia Minor. Because of his defiance, he was exiled to the island of Patmos, about twenty-five miles west of Ephesus. From this place of exile he wrote a letter to the seven leading churches of the region, a letter that actually expanded into a book. His *purpose* is to encourage persecuted Christians by telling them that their suffering will soon be over because they are now living in the last days when God will destroy Rome and establish his Kingdom on earth. The present wars and famines are signs that the end is near. His is a message of faith and hope for Christians undergoing extreme suffering. Stand firm! God will triumph! Christ is coming! "The time is at hand!"

The book of The Revelation begins to reveal its true meaning when we stop trying to apply it to an age other than its own and read it in the light of these first-century Roman persecutions. Equally necessary is some knowledge of the apocalyptic form in which it was written. The word "apocalyptic" means "unveil" or "reveal" and refers specifically to the revelation of truth about the end of history (eschatology). Speculation about this "end time" was very popular among the Jews in the time of Jesus, as we know from such books as Daniel and Enoch. Since Jesus borrowed certain concepts from this apocalyptic tradition in announcing his own message, it is not surprising to find Christians producing apocalypses of their own. The thirteenth chapter of Mark and the second chapter of Second Thessalonians are examples of how popular this form of literature became. We must understand that when John wrote a letter in apocalyptic form, he could assume that his readers would be very familiar with the apocalyptic "code."

All apocalyptic literature followed the same general pattern. According to this view, the power of evil (Satan) that is now in control of human history will soon be destroyed by the direct intervention of God, who will establish a new and glorious age in which his righteous followers will be rewarded. But before this can happen, evil must reach its height and seem to triumph utterly over good. When the situation is darkest, at precisely this moment, God will act and the dawn of the New Age will come! Nearly all apocalyptic literature relied heavily upon cryptic symbolic terms in which empires and individuals were pictured as beasts and monsters. Evil forces were described in strange visionary figures and forms, and mystic numbers always played an important role, especially the number seven.

In every sense, The Revelation is one of the finest examples in existence of an apocalypse. It opens with an encouraging letter to each of the seven churches (Rev., chs. 1 to 3) and then proves how the present age meets all the conditions of apocalyptic speculation. The breaking of

seven seals (Rev., chs. 4 to 7), the blowing of seven
trumpets (Rev., chs. 8 to 11), and the pouring out of
seven bowls of wrath (Rev., chs. 15 and 16) are the symbols
used by the author to describe all of the terrible woes that
have come upon the earth as a sign that evil is reaching
its height. The crowning blow and the certain sign that the
end is near is the appearance of the Antichrist, who de-
mands the worship that is due to God alone (Rev., chs. 12
to 14). The Antichrist is Nero, who is not named, but is
indicated in good apocalyptic fashion by a magic number,
"666." This represents the numerical value of the letters
in "Nero Caesar" when they are added together. Nero
had been dead thirty years when The Revelation was
written, but John pictures him coming back from the
"abyss" to which he had descended after death in order
to lead the hosts of evil. This is the sign of the end, for
when the last woes have taken place, all men will be
brought into judgment before God (Rev., chs. 17 to 20),
and the New Age will dawn (Rev., chs. 21 and 22). God
will send his Christ, evil will be destroyed, and a new
heaven and a new earth will be created. The description
of the heavenly Jerusalem descending to earth and the
people of God entering into it ranks high among the most
serenely beautiful passages in the Bible.

All of this is described in the typical cryptic language
of apocalyptic literature. In this case the language proved
a valuable "code," easily understood by the Christian
readers, but meaningless to the Romans. The writer hated
the Roman government and denounced its wickedness in
violent terms. Rome is a harlot, "drunk with the blood of
the saints"! We can imagine the joy of the Christians in
receiving such an incendiary book, written in prison and
sent in defiance of the hated enemy.

When The Revelation is set in its historical context and

the apocalyptic form is understood, most of the mystery surrounding the book disappears. It is simply a powerful message of encouragement to persecuted Christians who are told to remain strong in the faith because the end of all things is near. The righteous God is about to triumph over evil and establish his eternal Kingdom. It should be noted that the book served its original purpose well, comforting the Christians of Asia Minor and bringing them victoriously through their dreadful situation.

In one sense the book is of very little permanent value, because John's predictions proved utterly wrong. The evil Domitian was succeeded by five good emperors who befriended the Christians. Antichrist did not appear. The woes of the Christians gave way to unexpected blessings as the church grew and became materially powerful and influential. Rome did not fall, but grew in strength and continued to rule for centuries, finally becoming the guardian of the very church in whose name John had condemned it with such bitterness! The book is of some historical value in preserving one phase of Christian thought during the closing years of the first century, but as prophecy it was a dismal failure.

For the permanent value of the book we must look in another direction. The entire message is a glorious expression of faith that has stirred the hearts of readers in every generation. In the darkest days of the church's history, John was absolutely certain that nothing could destroy the cause of Christ. When the church's strength seemed weakest, John's faith in God was strongest. Though the forces of evil were ravaging the friends of God, John was able to encourage them by reminding them of the ultimate triumph of the righteous. In the face of hopeless defeat and destruction, he painted an immortal picture of the certain and glorious triumph of the Kingdom of God.

Seldom in the history of religious literature has there been such a declaration of faith. The preoccupation of later generations with the mystical language of The Revelation has been most unfortunate. Because of it, we have missed its exhilarating and undying message of faith:

> Then I saw a new heaven and a new earth; for the first heaven and the first earth had passed away, and the sea was no more. And I saw the holy city, new Jerusalem, coming down out of heaven from God, prepared as a bride adorned for her husband; and I heard a great voice from the throne saying, "Behold, the dwelling of God is with men. He will dwell with them, and they shall be his people, and God himself will be with them; he will wipe away every tear from their eyes, and death shall be no more, neither shall there be mourning nor crying nor pain any more, for the former things have passed away." And he who sat upon the throne said, "Behold, I make all things new." (Rev. 21:1-5.)

The voice of John echoes down across the centuries to remind us of one of the great convictions of our faith: God rules, and in his hands are the issues of our existence!

2. Problems

The problem of authorship in the case of The Revelation is complicated by the fact that there are so many "Johns" in the New Testament tradition. John the Baptist and John Zebedee both figure prominently in the ministry of Jesus. According to tradition, the Fourth Gospel, three letters, and The Revelation were all written by "John." From the early church fathers we know of "John the elder," who was prominent in the church at Ephesus at the beginning of the second century. It is not surprising that the

New Testament student often finds himself confused in trying to determine the authorship of these five "Johannine" documents.

We shall soon see that the Fourth Gospel and the three letters were all written by the same person, an unknown John who may have depended upon a source closely related to John Zebedee. The book of The Revelation was written by another unknown John, possibly John the elder, though he does not refer to himself by any such title. The fact that Second and Third John refer to "the elder" does not contradict this conclusion, since any elderly teacher could use this title of authority. For purposes of convenience, students often refer to the author of the Gospel and letters as "John the Evangelist," and to the author of The Revelation as "John the elder."

3. Outline

1. Preface (ch. 1:1–3)
2. The letter to the churches (chs. 1:4 to 3:22)
   a. The covering letter (ch. 1:4–20)
   b. Letters to seven churches (chs. 2:1 to 3:22)
3. Opening visions (chs. 4:1 to 5:14)
   a. Adoration of God (ch. 4:1–11)
   b. Adoration of the Lamb of God (ch. 5:1–14)
4. The woes of the seven seals (chs. 6:1 to 8:6)
5. The woes of the seven trumpets (chs. 8:7 to 11:19)
6. The coming of the Antichrist (chs. 12:1 to 14:20)
7. The woes of the seven bowls (chs. 15:1 to 16:21)
8. Visions of judgment (chs. 17:1 to 20:15)
9. The New Age (chs. 21:1 to 22:5)
10. Epilogue (ch. 22:6–21)

Chapter 20

James

1. Background

THE LETTER of James is a coat of many colors. It has been called a letter, a sermon, a book, and a manual of instruction. James, the brother of Jesus, James the apostle, and an unknown Greek teacher have been credited with its authorship. It is both a Jewish tract and a Christian homily. Some say it was written early to a specific group; others insist it was written late as a general letter to all Christians. Few documents in Christian history have given rise to as wide a variety of interpretations as this brief epistle.

Unfortunately, the letter gives few hints about its context and background. The opening salutation is the only place where the author makes any reference to himself: "James, a servant of God and of the Lord Jesus Christ." Strong tradition attributes the book to James, the brother of the Lord and the head of the church in Jerusalem. From all accounts we have of him, he was an effective leader who sternly insisted on obedience to the law. This letter was apparently written by just such a man, but there are two difficulties in accepting this traditional theory. First, no book in the New Testament tells us less about Jesus, yet who should be more interested in him than his own brother? Second, the book is written in such obvious Greek form, including familiarity with classical ideas and phrases, that it is difficult to believe that James, growing up in Nazareth with Jesus, could be responsible for it in its present form. About all we can say with certainty is that the document was written by a Christian teacher familiar with Judaism and Hellenism. The name "James" may have been placed at the beginning to lend stature to the work and to help it win acceptance among Christian readers.

The letter is addressed to "the twelve tribes in the dispersion," but the phrase is not to be taken literally. This is a symbolic designation meaning the church in its totality. For this reason, James is often described as a "catholic" or "general" epistle, intended for the church at large rather than for any particular community or person. The date of writing is difficult to ascertain, but certain internal evidence, including the writer's familiarity with other New Testament documents, leads us to suggest A.D. 100, or perhaps a little earlier, as the date of composition.

The writer's *purpose* is to provide a practical guide for the everyday life of Christian believers. Many persons are disappointed in James because it fails to plumb the depths of religious experience. The writer shows no interest in philosophy, theology, or devotional piety. On the contrary, he is concerned only with the very practical aspects of daily life, as demonstrated in his well-known definition of religion: "Religion that is pure and undefiled before God and the Father is this: to visit orphans and widows in their affliction, and to keep oneself unstained from the world" (James 1:27). The letter ignores the spiritual aspects of religion and views Christianity as a legalistic or ethical system. This is why some commentators believe it is a Jewish tract that has been slightly revised for the use of

Christians. But this is too radical a judgment. The New Testament writers had their experience of Christ in common, but they interpreted this experience in a wide variety of ways. As in our own time, there were many who were primarily interested in the ethical side of religion, seeking from it only a set of rules or laws for the "good life." James is the New Testament's outstanding example of this variety of religious interest. The document is Christian, not Jewish, but it is definitely one-sided, illustrating only one phase of the Christian life.

In a much-quoted comment, Martin Luther called James "that epistle of straw." By this he did not mean to condemn the letter as a whole, only its lack of theological content. The ethical qualities he enthusiastically commended: "I praise this epistle of James and consider it to be good, because it teaches no human doctrine at all and sternly declares the law of God." By itself, the letter gives an unbalanced picture of Christian faith, but as a part of the New Testament family it has served a useful function. New Christians in the ancient pagan world needed a great deal of practical instruction, just as Christians in every generation need to be reminded of the ethical demands of their religion, for "faith apart from works is dead."

The author's purpose may be clearly discerned in the contents and plan of his work. He offers a series of maxims or sayings in no obvious order or arrangement. Each saying, complete in itself, is related to other sayings only by minor associations of thought or language. A general summary of the contents is impossible because of this lack of ordered arrangement. It has been suggested that James was originally a "street-corner sermon" delivered by an itinerant Christian teacher. If so, the variety is intentional, for ancient sermons seldom developed one theme, but offered a wide variety of ideas in order to win and hold the attention of listeners.

Although a general theme is lacking, the book of James betrays two special interests of the author. One of these is his conviction that wealth is evil. In the Synoptic Gospels, Jesus warns against the dangers of riches because of the way in which material things tend to divert attention toward themselves and away from "the one thing needful." The author of James, however, regards wealth as evil in itself. He warns the rich man that he will pass away in the midst of his pursuits (James 1:9–11). Reminding the poor of all they have suffered, he cries out, "Is it not the rich who oppress you, is it not they who drag you into court? Is it not they who blaspheme that honorable name by which you are called?" (James 2:6–7). He tells the rich to weep and howl for the miseries that are coming upon them because of the way they have treated the laborers and the poor. (James 5:1–6.) We have no way of knowing why the author is so concerned about this problem, but he follows in a great tradition, echoing the prophet Amos, who cried out in protest against the rich who "sell the needy for a pair of shoes"!

Of much greater significance is this letter's emphasis on the relationship of faith and works. In what is probably the most famous passage in the book there is an apparent attack on Paul's great doctrine of justification by faith (James 2:14–26). "What does it profit, my brethren, if a man says he has faith but has not works? Can his faith save him?" In developing his argument, James points to Abraham and Rahab as examples. In his letter to the Romans, Paul had used Abraham as an outstanding illustration of one who was justified by faith. But James refutes this argument directly: "Was not Abraham our father justified by works, when he offered his son Isaac upon the altar? You see that faith was active along with his works, and faith was completed by works. . . . You see that a man is justified by works and not by faith alone."

The Letter to the Hebrews had cited Rahab's faith: "By faith Rahab the harlot did not perish with those who were disobedient." To this James replies, "In the same way was not also Rahab the harlot justified by works when she received the messengers and sent them out another way?" On the surface this seems to be a rejection of justification by faith, the doctrine around which so much New Testament thought revolves.

Paul, however, had never proclaimed faith apart from works. On the contrary, he insisted that the experience of faith always results in a new life of love and purity. He ends all his letters, even the most theological, with ethical counsel, knowing that those who had been reconciled to God through faith would desire specific instruction concerning works of love. Paul would be the first to agree that "faith by itself, if it has no works, is dead," and he would undoubtedly commend James for attacking those who were turning his doctrine into a religion without morality.

The unfortunate thing is that James misses the real point of the Christian religion when he treats it as a new kind of legalistic ethical system. According to his view, Christianity is superior to Judaism mainly because it has a superior law. Paul, on the other hand, and most of the other New Testament writers were able to see a more crucial difference. Jesus Christ brought to men first of all the possibility of entering into a new kind of relationship to God, a relationship of reconciliation made possible through faith. Those who are thus reconciled are motivated in a new way to live the good life. They want to obey the law, not in order to be saved, but because they have been saved. Morality thus springs from a prior and deeper religious experience, a fact that partly explains the uniqueness and power of the Christian life. James has performed a service in correcting those who misunderstood justification by faith, but he has misunderstood it himself at a deeper level and in a far more serious way.

2. Problems

We have interpreted the book of James as a Christian writing that expresses one important phase of thought in the life of the early church. But there remains the haunting problem of its relationship to Jewish sources. Although the form betrays a thorough familiarity with Greek phrases and ideas, the letter has borrowed heavily from Judaism in its interpretation of the Christian life. Has James depended on written or oral Jewish sources?

There is no way of answering with certainty, but some scholars are convinced that he used a "letter of Jacob," an older Jewish tract, as the basis for his own work. In Greek and in Hebrew, "James" and "Jacob" are the same word. Thus the opening words of the original source might have read, "Jacob, a servant of God, to the twelve tribes in the dispersion: Greeting." Such a document would be ideally suited for use by a Christian teacher who was writing to "dispersed" Christians on matters closely related to the law. This hypothesis is by no means universally accepted, but it does help explain many of the puzzling features of this epistle which, in spite of its narrow outlook, helps to meet the practical needs of Christians in every age.

3. Outline

1. Address (ch. 1:1)
2. Moral counsels (chs. 1:2 to 2:13)
3. Faith and works (ch. 2:14–26)
4. Christian words (ch. 3:1–18)
5. Moral counsels (chs. 4:1 to 5:12)
6. Practical advice (ch. 5:13–20)

Chapter 21

The Gospel of John

1. Background

THE GOSPEL of John is in many ways the masterpiece of the Bible. The author was one of those unique figures who combines rare talent with deep religious insight. In true artistic fashion, he has created a portrait of Jesus that is both simple and profound. This has been the favorite Gospel of countless millions of persons because of its direct and clear record of the life of Jesus. At the same time, the most learned scholars have called it "the profoundest of all writings." It has been described as a spiritual biography, a book of devotion, a theological treatise, and an inspired meditation. It is all these and more. The author has so skillfully blended historical fact with religious experience that the reader, seeking for the facts, finds himself sharing in the experience. In the fourth century, Jerome chose the eagle as the symbol for the Fourth Gospel. He chose well, for this is a majestic, soaring book.

A so-called Johannine problem arises, however, when we begin to compare this Gospel with the Synoptics. The author obviously knew the first three Gospels well, for he follows their general outline, supplementing and correcting it at certain vital points. In some places he has ob-

viously adopted incidents and even phrases from the other
Gospels; elsewhere he assumes that his readers already
know the essential facts about Jesus. But all of the material
has been so molded by his literary and religious genius that
his Gospel stands in splendid isolation from the others.

In recording the teaching of Jesus he omits the parables
and short sayings and substitutes long discourses on re-
curring themes, all cast in an allegorizing style in which
every phrase has a double meaning. The ministry expands
to three years in this Gospel, most of it taking place in
Jerusalem rather than Galilee. John knows nothing of the
"Messianic secret." Here Jesus openly declares his Messiah-
ship from the beginning, and others recognize him in this
role. In a radical departure from the Synoptics, John places
the Temple-cleansing at the beginning of the ministry and
the Last Supper on the day before Passover. He omits four
of the most important events in the life of Jesus, the
baptism, the temptation, the transfiguration, and the agony
in Gethsemane. There is no account of the Eucharist in
the upper room. New characters, such as Nicodemus and
the woman of Samaria, have long interviews with Jesus,
and the astounding miracle of the raising of Lazarus is
added and emphasized. In these and many other signifi-
cant ways the Fourth Gospel differs from the other three.

The main reason for these differences was noted as early
as A.D. 200 by Clement of Alexandria who said, "After the
other Evangelists had written down the facts of history,
John wrote a spiritual Gospel." What he means is that
John's intention is not to add another "historical" Gospel,
but to interpret the career of Jesus in spiritual or theologi-
cal terms. This explains his method of taking only a few
events from the life of Jesus and elaborating upon their
meaning, always relating them to Jesus in such a way as
to show more clearly how he is "the Christ, the Son of
God." The Synoptic Gospels, as we have seen, all contain

a certain amount of theological interpretation, but John has carried this to the extreme. His main interest is in the theological or spiritual meaning of the words and acts of Jesus.

This interest is obvious from the opening verse to the last. He sets the theme of his Gospel in a matchless prologue in which Jesus is presented as the incarnate Word of God. The story of the public ministry is built around a framework of seven miracle stories and a series of discourses and dialogues, all clearly illustrating John's interpretive purpose. An entire chapter, for example, is used to describe the healing of a blind man so that the author can exhibit Jesus as the one who brings sight to all who are spiritually blind. The raising of Lazarus becomes the perfect vehicle for presenting Christ as one who brings new life to all those who are spiritually dead. It is extremely difficult at times, as in the interview with Nicodemus, to determine where history ends and allegory begins. The upper room discourses are so important to this writer that they become a separate section of his book. He concludes with the most dramatic and vivid Passion narrative in any of our records and emphasizes the resurrection as God's climactic revelation through the Word made flesh.

One of the unique qualities of this Gospel is the author's desire to probe and express the innermost thoughts of Jesus himself. In the Synoptics we look at the story of Jesus from the outside, but John enables us to see it from within the consciousness of Jesus. He is not so much interested in the words of Jesus as he is in Jesus' actual thoughts and intentions. This gives rise to a style that is totally unlike the Synoptics. He uses simple words, the repetition of key ideas, and short sentences. These are all used to create long discourses in which veiled language conveys rich spiritual truth. One of the reasons why this Gospel has always appealed to both the simple and the scholarly is that nearly every word and phrase has a simple direct meaning behind which lurks a hidden meaning so profound that it carries even the most intelligent reader out beyond his depth. In every case the author's intention is to reveal the inner consciousness of Jesus, thus making it possible for us to know "the Son" in the deep places of his own spirit. We might summarize this unique quality by saying that the Synoptics give us Jesus as he was known to others whereas John gives us Jesus as he was known to himself.

Unfortunately, the identity of the spiritual genius who wrote this Gospel remains one of the unsolved puzzles of New Testament study. Until the nineteenth century the book was almost universally accepted as the work of John Zebedee, one of the Twelve. It was believed that he had migrated to Ephesus in Asia Minor and as a very old man had written his reminiscences of the life of Jesus. This view adds to the value of this Gospel by making it the work of one of the intimate disciples of Jesus, "the disciple whom Jesus loved." A great deal of evidence can be summoned to support this view, including the testimony of the early church fathers (after the second century) and the nature of the Gospel itself, which shows a remarkable knowledge of details in the life of Jesus and in the geography of Palestine. In addition, this writer does not hesitate to correct the Synoptics on such important matters as the date of the Last Supper and crucifixion. Most modern scholars are convinced that John is correct in placing these on the day before Passover.

On the other hand, the negative evidence is so strong that even the most conservative critics now claim for John only some indirect part in the writing of this Gospel. No single factor is decisive, but the cumulative weight of evidence is very strong. (*a*) The life of Jesus is not described

in a way that suggests the reporting of an immediate disci-
ple. (*b*) It is not likely that a Galilean disciple would be
so anxious to cast Jesus into a mold of Hellenistic theology.
(*c*) The Fourth Gospel in most points is far removed from
the actual conditions at the time of Jesus. (*d*) Although
written in isolation, as we have seen, the Gospel is never-
theless dependent upon the Synoptics at many points.
John's greatest contribution is in the interpretation of facts
already known. (*e*) The Johannine authorship is not men-
tioned in the early documents until A.D. 180. (*f*) John
would hardly refer to himself as "the beloved disciple."
(*g*) Modern scholarship tends to date the Gospel near the
first decade of the second century, A.D. 100–110. If this
date is accurate, it is scarcely likely that John Zebedee
would be able to compose this literary and religious mas-
terpiece at such an advanced age. Other evidence could be
summoned, but this is enough to show how the theory of
Johannine authorship has been largely undermined and
rejected.

Fortunately, the religious value of the book does not
depend upon our knowledge of the author. He may have
kept himself anonymous on purpose, feeling that his work
should go out on the authority of the Holy Spirit rather
than be identified with any particular man. Whoever he
was, he ranks along with Paul as one of the two greatest
minds of the early church. He demonstrates a thorough
knowledge of Judaism as well as of the Greek philosophical
concepts into which he casts much of his thought. In addi-
tion, the discovery of the Dead Sea scrolls has brought to
light his unusually intimate knowledge of sectarian Juda-
ism (the Essenes). In a real sense this great author repre-
sents a synthesis of traditional Judaism, Hellenism, and
sectarian Judaism.

Certain controversial interests are apparent in this Gos-
pel apart from the author's desire to present a spiritual

interpretation of Jesus. (*a*) He is anxious to subordinate John the Baptist to Jesus in opposition to the sect that had been founded by those who were convinced that John was superior to Jesus. This is especially evident in the opening chapter. (*b*) He opposes synagogue Judaism, which by the end of the first century was in open conflict with the Christian movement. In his Gospel the enemies of Jesus become simply "the Jews," reflecting the later controversy and not the actual conditions in the time of Jesus when the opposition came from certain Jews and not "the Jews" in general. (*c*) He indirectly refutes the claims of the Gnostic movement, which became such a problem to the early church. Gnosticism attempted to transform Christianity into a speculative system that emphasized the importance of secret "knowledge" and turned Jesus into a heavenly being entirely unrelated to this world. As we will see, First John was written to counteract this position, and we can scarcely doubt that a similar motive runs through the Gospel.

Most important of all are the two themes that stand out as the main burden of the author's thought. His *purpose* in writing is to present a religious interpretation of Jesus, a spiritual Gospel to supplement the historical Gospels that were already available. He states the two principal reasons for doing this in a famous passage at the end of the book: "Now Jesus did many other signs in the presence of the disciples, which are not written in this book; but these are written that you may believe that Jesus is the Christ, the Son of God, and that believing you may have [eternal] life in his name" (John 20:30–31; ch. 21 is an appendix). By his own admission, his intention is to present (*a*) Jesus as the Son of God and (*b*) eternal life as the priceless gift that the Son makes available to men.

The first theme is that Jesus is the Son of God and knew himself to be the Son of God from the very beginning.

This is one reason why the Johannine Jesus seems so different from the Jesus known by those who have just come from the Synoptics. In the majestic prologue (John 1:1–18), we do not meet Jesus as a babe in a manger, but as the incarnate Word (Logos) of God. This means that he is the incarnate expression of the divine revealing activity of God that has been at work from the beginning of time. Later in the Gospel, Jesus expresses his own awareness of this unique relationship to God in several famous "I am" passages. This is what Jesus knew himself to be in the depths of his own being: "I am the bread of life. . . . I am the light of the world. . . . I am the door of the sheep. . . . I am the good shepherd. . . . I am the true vine. . . . I am the resurrection and the life. . . . I am the way, and the truth, and the life." He also refers to himself as "the Son," not the "Son of man" of the Synoptics, but the Son of God who is in a relationship of love and dependent trust with the Father. "The Son" is an expression of the deep consciousness of God that was the very secret of Jesus' being. He also tells his disciples that he and the Father "are one," thus emphasizing the sense of unity that he feels with the essential being of God.

In these and other ways the author develops his central theme. He has been called "the historian of the consciousness of Jesus" because of his particular interest in the inner life of Jesus. But this interest grows out of his own conviction that the mission and message of Jesus are grounded in Jesus' own awareness of Sonship with the Father. Thus he writes in order that others may know and believe that "Jesus is the Christ, the Son of God."

His second theme is the eternal life that the Son of God brings to men. The Kingdom (Reign) of God that was the theme of Jesus' teaching in the Synoptics becomes in John "eternal life." By this he does not mean some future event or place, but a present quality of life that is above time and physical death. "This is eternal life, that they know thee the only true God, and Jesus Christ whom thou hast sent." (John 17:3.) Jesus did not mean "knowing" God intellectually, but knowing him in an act that involved the whole life and personality of the individual, his total being. Eternal life is thus unconditional love of God, selfless obedience to him, fulfilling fellowship with him.

This means that eternal life is present and not future. It exists "now," whenever a person chooses to enter into this new relationship with God. At the same time it is timeless, eternal not only in duration but in quality. It also involves judgment as a present experience. "This is the judgment, that the light has come into the world, and men loved darkness rather than light, because their deeds were evil." (John 3:19.) "Truly, I say to you, he who hears my word and believes him who sent me, has eternal life; he does not come into judgment, but has passed from death to life." (John 5:24.) Thus the judgment is a present spiritual experience in which we choose or reject God *now*.

Like a mighty symphony, this Gospel presents these two themes in an infinite variety of movements and moods. Through it all there is the pervading presence of Jesus, revealing to us the deep places of his own spirit, the inner consciousness that makes it possible for him to act and speak as the Son of God. One of the greatest scholars of modern times once said, "I have more love for Saint John's Gospel than for any other book." Many who read it and live with it will understand and agree.

2. *Problems*

Most scholars are certain that the present Gospel of John contains two passages that were not part of the original work. One of these is the account of the woman taken in adultery (John 7:53 to 8:11). This is omitted in all the earliest manuscripts, is missing from many of the later ones, and appears in some manuscripts of Luke. It interrupts the order of John and differs from him in style and thought. It is generally agreed that it is an authentic incident from the life of Jesus that came to a later editor of John as a stray fragment of tradition. We do not know why the Synoptics omitted it, but we may be grateful to the editor of the Fourth Gospel who has preserved it in John.

The other addition is the closing chapter, which is almost universally viewed as an appendix added by a later editor (John, ch. 21). As we have noted, the book comes to a close at the end of ch. 20. Then we find ourselves in the midst of a resurrection account whose character is unlike the rest of the book. In itself the chapter is very beautifully written and may have come from the same source that preserved Luke's story of the journey to Emmaus. Apart from these two additions, the Gospel of John is usually viewed as a unity that has been preserved with a remarkable degree of accuracy.

3. Outline

Prologue (ch. 1:1–18)
1. Preparation (ch. 1:19–51)
2. The early ministry (chs. 2:1 to 6:71)
3. The growing conflict (chs. 7:1 to 12:50)
4. Jesus and the Twelve (chs. 13:1 to 17:26)
5. The Passion and death (chs. 18:1 to 19:42)
6. The Resurrection (ch. 20:1–31)
Appendix (ch. 21)

Chapter 22

The Letters of John

1. Background

THE LETTERS of John were written to combat a dangerous perversion of Christianity called Gnosticism, which appears behind the scenes in other New Testament documents but stands out here in bold relief. Its name comes from the Greek word for "knowledge" or "wisdom" and refers to secret knowledge necessary for salvation. According to this view, the material world is evil and the physical body is a prison for the soul. All of life is a struggle between the darkness of this world and the light of a higher world. Man's salvation depends upon secret and esoteric knowledge that he receives from a heavenly redeemer or "light bringer." Those who possess this knowledge become part of a cult or secret society whose members look upon themselves as superior to "ordinary" men, regularly participating in mysterious and magical rites understood only by the elect.

Gnosticism became strong in the first two centuries and tried to turn the church into an exclusive society built around Christ, as the revealer of secret knowledge, who came to help men escape from this life. Because of his divine nature, Christ was totally unrelated to this world of darkness and evil. He only *seemed* to have a physical body that suffered and died. Hence, these persons were often called Docetists or "Seemists." Because they did not believe in the idea of sin, they rejected the moral law as belonging to an inferior stage of religion. At almost every point they altered the portrait of Jesus that appears in the Gospels and forced his teaching to fit their own point of view. Their exclusiveness and their scorn of ethics are the complete opposite of the spirit of The Acts and the letters of Paul. If Gnosticism had prevailed, Christianity as we know it would have disappeared.

For this reason, the church leaders summoned all their strength to destroy the monstrous heresy. Even in Paul's time the movement was making itself felt, as we see from his letter to the Colossians. The Fourth Gospel also was written with these heretics in mind. This Gospel, more than any other, is interested in the divinity of Jesus, yet John is also eager to oppose the Docetists by proving Christ's full humanity. Thus Jesus "became flesh and dwelt among us," wept at the death of Lazarus, and thirsted on the cross. Now, in the Johannine letters the same great writer faces the heresy directly and seeks to destroy it. His *purpose* in all three letters is to combat Gnosticism by confirming his readers in the true fundamentals of Christian faith.

Third John is a very brief personal note written to Gaius, a man of some means, who followed the practice of receiving and caring for the traveling missionaries who were still prominent in the life of the church. Taking their example from the teaching of Jesus (Matt. 10:8–11,40), these itinerant preachers depended for support on the hospitality of persons in the churches they visited. In his note, John encourages Gaius to continue his practice of entertaining such travelers, and he warns him of impending trouble in the church. A man called Diotrephes, obviously spreading the false teaching of the Gnostics, was refusing hospitality to the authentic traveling teachers. Moreover, he had been slanderous and rude, undoubtedly seeking sole authority in the church. In his letter, John asks Gaius to show respect for all visitors who come proclaiming the truth of Christ. Meanwhile, he states his intention of appearing before long and dealing fittingly with the defiant troublemaker.

Second John is also a short note, this time addressed to the church of which Gaius is a member. The church as a whole is warned against false teachers, "men who will not acknowledge the coming of Jesus Christ in the flesh; such a one is the deceiver and the antichrist" (II John 7). This is a direct reference to the Docetists who were apparently gaining in strength. In opposition to their teaching, John briefly reviews the "true" doctrine of Christ, and ends with a warning: "If any one comes to you and does not bring this doctrine, do not receive him into the house or give him any greeting; for he who greets him shares his wicked work" (II John 10–11).

First John is a longer letter handling in greater detail the problems raised by the same Gnostic heresy. The two shorter notes contain little of theological value, and the question has often been raised as to why they were preserved and included in the New Testament canon. It is probably because they accompanied the longer letter when it was originally sent out and thus came to be viewed as an integral part of John's response to a dangerous situation. First John was probably intended as a pastoral letter to be read to the churches in the area affected by the heresy. It has been treasured by the church in every generation because of its clear and moving description of the ultimate and unchanging elements in the Christian faith. As one scholar has said, "No book has ever been written which takes us nearer to the very heart of our religion."

John develops his message around two very simple themes: (*a*) God's love and (*b*) brotherly love as the test of religion. He emphasizes the first in opposition to the claim of the Gnostic teachers that theirs is a higher religion based upon a superior truth, and the second in opposition to their exclusiveness.

One verse in First John has been much quoted by Christians in every age: "God is love." This principal theme is elaborated in many ways, but the main emphasis is always upon the ultimate nature of God's revelation of himself in Jesus Christ. Because of his love, God has revealed himself in Christ and continues to witness to the truth of Christ in the experience of the believer. There can be no higher revelation, no higher truth, than that already made manifest in Jesus Christ. "In this the love of God was made manifest among us, that God sent his only Son into the world, so that we might live through him." (I John 4:9.) This love witnesses to itself within our experience so that we no longer have to seek a higher "knowledge" of the truth. Something deep within us responds to God's revelation of himself in Christ, giving us a sense of assurance and certainty that no longer leaves any doubt. This inward witness of the Spirit is infinitely superior to the witness of men. "If we receive the testimony of men, the testimony of God is greater; for this is the testimony of God that he has borne witness to his Son." (I John 5:9.) God's love is such a living reality to this writer that every page of his letter seems to reflect the actual presence of God.

With unerring insight, John also knows how brotherly love inevitably grows out of man's experience of the divine love. For this reason, love for the brethren can be used as a test of "true religion." He who says he is "in the light," but hates his brother is still in the darkness, walking with blinded eyes. The true message from the beginning is that we should love one another. Anyone who does not love his brother is not of God. "Beloved, let us love one another; for love is of God, and he who loves is born of God and knows God. He who does not love does not know God; for God is love." (I John 4:7–8.)

In this way, the writer repeats and relates his two vital themes, God's love for man, and man's love for his brothers. The early Christians who heard his message must have seen the infinite superiority of such a revelation over the esoteric knowledge and arrogance of Gnosticism. John stated the issues so clearly and meaningfully that his letter has always been treasured by all Christians who love one another because they have first known the love of God.

We have assumed throughout the preceding discussion that the three letters all come from the hand of John the Evangelist. This is the judgment of the majority of modern scholars, who emphasize the similarities of thought and style between the Gospel and the letters. Even the casual reader will note the typical Johannine ideas and concepts as well as the repeated use of words like "truth," "light," "life," "witness," and "love." Those who doubt the common authorship of the Gospel and letters seek some clue to the problem in the two shorter letters in which the writer identifies himself as "the elder." But this reference is of little value, since this title was used for many older teachers in the early church as a sign of authority and respect. We are on more solid ground in assigning these letters to the great unknown author of the Gospel who probably wrote them about the same time, A.D. 100–110.

Were the letters written before or after the Gospel?

This question has been hotly debated without any general agreement on the answer. First John and the Gospel are closely related, but the letter has a purpose and a stature all its own. Whether written before or after, it is definitely a supplement to the Gospel, setting forth the practical ethical demands that are implicit in the larger work. It has been often noted that the Fourth Gospel keeps the ethical teaching of Jesus "in the shadow." The letter is extremely valuable, therefore, in setting forth the specific ethical demands of the Gospel's deeper religious principles. Taken together, the Gospel and First John constitute one of the richest deposits of spiritual truth in the Christian religion. Both reveal through Jesus Christ the way to God, the truth about God, the light of God, and both are filled with the same sense of awe and holy surprise at the wonder of God's love. "See what love the Father has given us, that we should be called the children of God; and so we are." (I John 3:1.)

2. Problems

The King James Version of First John contains a verse that has caused a great deal of difficulty among translators and commentators: "For there are three that bear record in heaven, the Father, the Word, and the Holy Ghost: and these three are one" (I John 5:7). This verse appears in no ancient Greek manuscript, nor is it cited by any early Greek writer. Of all the versions, only the Latin contained it and only in some later editions. It is the one verse in the New Testament that is entirely spurious and has now been omitted from every good text. It is interesting to note, however, how the reference to "three witnesses" in the true text prompted a fourth-century scribe to add his own Trinitarian interpretation. This might lead us to wonder whether the same type of interpolation has occurred less obviously in other places in other "standard" versions of our Bible.

3. Outlines

FIRST JOHN
1. Introduction (ch. 1:1–4)
2. Light vs. darkness (chs. 1:5 to 2:17)
3. Truth vs. falsehood (ch. 2:18–29)
4. Children of God vs. children of the devil (ch. 3:1–10)
5. Brotherly love (chs. 3:11 to 5:12)
6. Conclusion (ch. 5:13–21)

SECOND JOHN
1. Greeting (vs. 1–3)
2. Summons to love (vs. 4–6)
3. Warning against error (vs. 7–11)
4. Conclusion (vs. 12–13)

THIRD JOHN
1. Greeting (v. 1)
2. Praise of Gaius (vs. 2–8)
3. Condemnation of Diotrephes (vs. 9–11)
4. Conclusion (vs. 12–15)

Chapter 23

Jude and Second Peter

1. Background

THE TWO books in the New Testament that are chronologically last are very brief and of little religious value. Many have suggested that they do not belong in the New Testament at all, but they obviously met some pressing need in the early church. They are so closely related to each other that Second Peter is essentially a revision of Jude, with some additions to make it suitable for a new situation.

Both are addressed to Christians caught in the controversy with the Gnostics, but when Jude and Second Peter were written the movement had become widespread and extreme in its opposition to the "accepted faith." These writers feel the necessity of contending "for the faith which was once for all delivered to the saints." The specific problem they face is that of gross immorality arising from the Gnostic rejection of moral law. Some of the heretics believed that their superior knowledge raised them to a level of existence beyond mundane moral responsibility. They evidently indulged the body with all its appetites and generally became a scandal in the churches and communities where they lived. The *purpose* of Jude and Second Peter is to combat the immorality of Gnosticism, which presented a serious threat to the second-century church.

Jude was written about A.D. 125 by an unknown teacher who used the epistolary form, though he intended his work as a general tract for all Christians. After pleading with his readers to hold fast to the accepted faith, he launches into a polemic against the immorality of the Gnostics. They "defile the flesh, reject authority," "boldly carouse together," and act with the instinct of irrational animals. They are like "waterless clouds, carried along by winds; fruitless trees in late autumn, twice dead, uprooted; wild waves of the sea, casting up the foam of their own shame; wandering stars for whom the nether gloom of darkness has been reserved for ever" (Jude 12–13). They are "grumblers, malcontents, following their own passions, loud-mouthed boasters, flattering people to gain advantage" (Jude 16). In language reminiscent of the Old Testament prophets, the author paints this picture of their immorality and points out the fearful consequences of their disobedience.

As for Christians, they are to build themselves up in their most holy faith, praying in the Holy Spirit, keeping themselves in the love of God, and waiting for the mercy of the Lord Jesus Christ. Some of the heretics they may be able to save, others can only be feared and pitied. Jude ends his letter with a benediction that is one of the most beautiful in the New Testament.

> Now to him who is able to keep you from falling and to present you without blemish before the presence of his glory with rejoicing, to the only God, our Savior through Jesus Christ our Lord, be glory, majesty, dominion, and authority, before all time and now and for ever. Amen. (Jude 24–24.)

Second Peter was written about A.D. 150 by an unknown author who used Jude as a model for his own letter. The Gnostic heresy was even more destructive when he wrote, so he condemns the false teachers at greater length and with increased vehemence. After an opening chapter praising the traditional faith as the way of salvation, he condemns the same immoral practices that were a problem for the writer of Jude. In fact, he uses that letter as his own second chapter, incorporating not only its ideas but many of its words and phrases. To this he adds a chapter in which he defends the Second Coming of Christ, a teaching that had been prominent in the early church but which began to fade in the second century. This was partly due to the long delay in fulfillment: "Where is the promise of his coming? For ever since the fathers fell asleep, all things have continued as they were from the beginning" (II Peter 3:4). This was the complaint that the author of Second Peter tries to answer by reviving the old confidence in the visible and immediate return of Christ. The Gnostic teachers were sowing seeds of doubt on this matter, but Second Peter insists that their skepticism is a certain sign of the nearness of the end. The new heavens and a new earth are coming soon! "Therefore, beloved, since you wait for these, be zealous to be found by him without spot or blemish, and at peace." (II Peter 3:14.)

These letters give us glimpses of a serious problem faced by the second-century church, but they are of little religious value. Obviously on a level below that of most of the New Testament, they were probably included in the canon because of their usefulness in meeting an immediate problem. Underlying both letters, however, there is one assumption that is of great value to Christians in every generation. Both authors refute the common idea that religious beliefs are of little consequence in daily life. They

insist that a man's convictions are of vital importance be-
cause they ultimately determine the way he acts and how
he lives. The false beliefs of the Gnostics led them into
immorality. The true beliefs of the Christians, on the other
hand, enable them to live in purity and love, "without
spot or blemish." In this insistence on the necessity of
sound religion as a basis for sound living, these letters meet
a universal need in man's experience.

2. Problems

The problem of authorship is perplexing in the case of
both Jude and Second Peter. The author of the former
calls himself "Jude, a servant of Jesus Christ and brother
of James," but both names are very common and do not
afford any clue to his real identity. Second Peter, on the
contrary, claims in no uncertain terms to be by the apostle
Peter. This claim is stated directly and implied in several
passages, including a reference to the transfiguration. The
evidence that Peter did not write the letter is overwhelm-
ing, however. It is a late work, based on Jude, and not
even mentioned in any of our records until the end of the
second century. Peter's name was used by many writers in
these early years and we know of a Gospel of Peter, an
Apocalypse of Peter, and the Acts of Peter, as well as this
brief letter. For this author, Peter stood as the symbol of
orthodoxy. He therefore did not hesitate to send forth a
letter in Peter's name, though who the actual author was
we have no way of knowing.

3. *Outline*

JUDE

1. Introduction (vs. 1–4)
2. Errors of the heretics (vs. 5–16)
3. A call to faith (vs. 17–23)
4. Benediction (vs. 24–25)

SECOND PETER

1. Introduction (ch. 1:1–2)
2. A call to faith (ch. 1:3–21)
3. Errors of the heretics (ch. 2:1–22)
4. The Second Coming (ch. 3:1–17)
5. Benediction (ch. 3:18)

Chapter 24

The New Testament Canon

1. Background

MODERN CHRISTIANS think of the New Testament as the authoritative Christian Scripture. But why were these twenty-seven documents chosen as "authoritative" and not others? Who made the decision? For quite some time the early Christians had no intention of using any other collection of sacred writings than the Old Testament, which was the Bible of the early church. What were the motives that led them to form a scripture of their own? These and other questions are related to the general problem of the New Testament canon.

The word "canon," which originally meant a "reed" or "measuring rod," came to mean "standard" or "rule." Hence we speak of the canon as the collection of twenty-seven books that became the "standard" authority in matters of faith and life. Modern Christians tend to forget the original need for such a standard or authoritative collection because they have lost sight of the other writings that appeared in the earliest days of the church.

The books in the New Testament are only a fragment of a larger and much varied body of literature created by the early Christians. A great deal has been lost, while some is preserved only in quotations from other books. Much is included in collections of early writings from the apostolic fathers and the apologists. How much material was produced we have no way of knowing, but recent discoveries continue to broaden our horizons. An example is the much discussed Gospel of Thomas that was discovered in Egypt in 1945.

The selection of a standard scripture out of this vast amount of written material was not the work of any individual or group. As a matter of fact, it is a difficult process to describe because it took place gradually over a long period of time. Various churches accepted different segments of the available writings as "standard" until the middle of the second century, when a decisive step was taken by Marcion, a famous heretic. This energetic teacher and organizer rejected the authority of the Old Testament and attempted to replace it with a Christian scripture made up of ten letters of Paul's and the Gospel of Luke. This Marcion Bible was rejected by the church, but it helped convince church leaders that an authoritative scripture was needed. The growing strength of the Gnostic heresies and the increasing number of fantastic and spurious "gospels" made it even more imperative.

Some of the documents were accepted from the beginning by common agreement. The four Gospels, the letters of Paul, the book of The Acts, First Peter, and First John all appear on the earliest lists that have come down to us. There was no general agreement on the others, however, until three rather nebulous criteria were gradually applied. (a) The writing had to be associated with one of the apostles. At first the church insisted that authoritative documents be written by apostles, but this would have excluded two of the Gospels, so the rule was modified to include books that were in the apostolic tradition. (*b*) The fact that a book was treasured and regularly used in one or more of the leading churches helped it gain acceptance. (*c*) Only those books were accepted which taught the accepted doctrine. This was extremely important, since the writings were used as weapons in the conflict with the heresies that were threatening every area of the church's life.

These criteria were very difficult to apply, and many books remained on the disputed list for some time. Hebrews and The Revelation eventually won their place, but only with great difficulty. The Revelation was almost lost when other apocalyptic types of writing were completely discredited. The last five documents to be admitted to the canon made their way into it only with the greatest difficulty. These were Second and Third John, James, Jude, and Second Peter. How many books were dropped along the way we do not know, but many were in the running for a long time. Examples of these are the letter of Barnabas, First Clement, and the Shepherd of Hermas.

We know from Christian writings that there were still several "canons" recognized in the church during the third century. All agreed on the major documents, but disagreed widely on the disputed books. Finally, one of the foremost leaders in the church, Bishop Athanasius of Alexandria, issued a list of accepted books in his annual Easter letter to the churches in his diocese. The list included precisely the twenty-seven books that we have come to know as our New Testament today. This was in the year A.D. 367, and from this time the canon was pretty generally accepted throughout the church, although church councils continued to debate various related issues for many years.

It usually comes as something of a shock when we first discover the rather fortuitous way in which the selection of these supremely important documents was made. How can we be sure that the final choice was the best one? Two factors supply the answer to this important question: (*a*) the intrinsic value of the books; (*b*) the presence of the Holy Spirit in the life of the early church.

We are indeed fortunate that the selection took place over a long period of time, for this meant that the intrinsic worth of the documents could be generally recognized. It is always extremely difficult to evaluate a work of literature when it first appears. Some that are most popular at first prove worthless. Others, scarcely noticed in their own time, become classics. The documents that were selected for our New Testament survived this test of time, retaining their freshness and becoming richer with the passing of the years. How well this process worked may be seen by comparing any of our present Gospels with the so-called Gospel of Thomas that caused so much excitement when it was first discovered. We were told that it was a "fifth Gospel" which would assume a place of high authority in the life of the church. But already we realize that it is an inferior work by every standard, a Gnostic writing that tries to fit Jesus into the patterns of the author's esoteric preconceptions. There is, in contrast, a self-authenticating quality about the documents of our New Testament that commend them to any thoughtful reader. As one interpreter aptly put it, "The church, in the end, selected those writings which had already selected themselves."

The other factor that cannot be overlooked in any survey of the New Testament canon is the presence of the Holy Spirit in the life of the early church. This is a difficult thing to describe to those who have not been privileged to participate in a fellowship vividly aware of the presence of the living God. Our book of The Acts and the letters of Paul give us ample testimony of the way in which the early

Christians left themselves "open" to the guidance of the Spirit. They were guided by the Holy Spirit, led by the Holy Spirit, and filled with the Holy Spirit. What this means is that they had a vivid awareness of the presence of God, an awareness that was heightened by the vitality of the life-sharing fellowship of love in which they were joined. As we review the history of the church we find a great deal of evidence of this divine Presence, but none more convincing than the quality of the books finally selected for the New Testament canon. These are not only great works of literature but they plumb the depths of Christian experience as no other books in existence. Here we meet the Creator who is the loving Father, the Son who became Redeemer and Lord, and the Holy Spirit who continues to warm the hearts of faithful believers. In every document we feel the holy joy and breath-taking surprise of those who had found their existence transformed by the saving act of God in Jesus Christ. All this is a sign to us that the Spirit of God was guiding the mind of the early church in the supremely important task of choosing its Scripture.

We are hearing a great deal in modern times about the need for the recovery of spiritual vitality in the churches of Christendom. Surely that vitality will come when we interpret and apply the truth of the New Testament books under the guidance of the living and ever-present God who led the early Christians to choose these books out of all the rest.

Appendix

Suggestions for Study and Discussion

CHAPTER ONE: *God's Good News*

1. Obtain as many translations of the New Testament as possible. Read several familiar passages in each (e.g., Matt., chs. 5 to 7; John, ch. 1; I Cor., ch. 13), and compare the style of the various editions.
2. Which translation do you consider most useful for serious study? Which for devotional reading?
3. Try to describe in a brief paragraph or two the nature of your Christian experience. What difference does Christ make in your life? As you study the New Testament, try to decide whether the writers are describing Christian experience as you understand it.
4. Examine the order of the New Testament books. Can you discern any purpose in this order? If the Gospels were written later than Paul's letters, why were they placed first?
5. What was the original language of the New Testament? What problems arise when religious ideas are translated from one language to another?

CHAPTER TWO: *First Thessalonians*

1. Read First Thessalonians, using the outline as a guide.

2. Try to discover in the text the reasons why Paul wrote this letter. Note especially chs. 3:3–5; 3:13; 4:13.

3. Locate Thessalonica on a map of the ancient world, remembering that this was one of Paul's first congregations in "Europe."

4. Read chs. 4:13 to 5:11, noting Paul's discussion of the Second Coming of Jesus. What value does this doctrine have for modern Christians?

5. Read Paul's defense of himself in ch. 2:1–18. What were his enemies teaching that he opposed so strongly?

CHAPTER THREE: *Second Thessalonians*

1. Read Second Thessalonians.

2. Note the strong resemblance of this letter to First Thessalonians. Do they seem to be written by the same person?

3. Read ch. 2:1–12. How had Paul's teaching on the Second Coming been misunderstood by the Thessalonians?

4. Write a brief paraphrase of Paul's new argument concerning the Second Coming, ch. 2:1–12. Many scholars doubt that Paul wrote this passage. Do you agree?

5. Note ch. 3:10, Paul's famous "principle of work." Write a brief statement on the subject of honest work as an element in the Christian life.

CHAPTER FOUR: *Galatians*

1. Read Galatians aloud. Imagine yourself hearing it as a member of a congregation. What would your reaction be?

2. Chapters 1 and 2 have been called Paul's autobiography. Read them and list the important facts about Paul's life which they reveal.

3. Locate Galatia on the map. Do you think the "Gala-

tians" of this letter belonged to churches in the north or south of the province? Remember, scholars cannot agree.

4. Record the number of times Paul mentions freedom in this letter. Why did he emphasize this idea so strongly?

5. Summarize Paul's argument in chs. 3 and 4. What does he mean by "justification by faith"?

CHAPTER FIVE: *First Corinthians*

1. Read First Corinthians, noting how the argument moves from subject to subject, almost at random.

2. Read Paul's reference to an earlier letter in ch. 5:9. Do we have any evidence of this letter?

3. Locate Corinth on a map, noting its strategic importance.

4. Read chs. 13 and 15, two of the most famous passages in the New Testament. What is Paul's main point in each?

5. Read ch. 8 and notice the classic statement of Christian conduct in v. 13. How does this principle apply to modern Christians?

CHAPTER SIX: *Second Corinthians*

1. Read Second Corinthians in the following order: chs. 10 to 13 and chs. 1 to 9.

2. List the evidence for regarding our present Second Corinthians as two separate letters.

3. Note the autobiographical quality of "the angry letter" (chs. 10 to 13). What facts about Paul's life do these chapters reveal? Compare with Galatians, chs. 1 and 2.

4. What is Paul's main purpose in sending the "letter of reconciliation"? (II Cor., chs. 1 to 9). List verses that reveal this purpose.

5. The two Corinthian letters have been called Paul's "church letters." List the problems discussed in these letters which are vital in the conduct of church life.

Chapter Seven: *Romans*

1. Read Romans in a modern translation, using the outline and following the argument carefully.
2. List several reasons why the Roman church figured so prominently in Paul's missionary plans. Why did he exert so much care in composing this letter?
3. Describe in one concise paragraph what Paul means by "justification by faith." How is this related to Christian experience as we understand it today?
4. Read chs. 7 and 8. Do they properly describe the real problem of sin and salvation?
5. Read ch. 12. What is the most important thing about the Christian ethical life as Paul describes it here?

Chapter Eight: *Colossians*

1. Read Colossians, keeping in mind the "false teaching" that Paul was opposing.
2. Write a brief description of the "Colossian heresy." Note that it will reappear in a more acute form in later New Testament writings.
3. This has been called Paul's "Christological letter." What are the important things he says about Christ?
4. Locate Colossae on the map. How was this church related to Paul?
5. Read chs. 3:5 to 4:6. Why does Paul end nearly every letter with ethical teaching?

Chapter Nine: *Philemon*

1. Read Philemon as a personal note from Paul to a man of some influence. Do you think Paul used the best approach?

2. Describe the situation that caused Paul to write this note.
3. Paul has been criticized for not attacking the evils of slavery in this letter. How would you defend him?

CHAPTER TEN: *Philippians*

1. Read Philippians, remembering that it may have been Paul's "farewell address" from prison in Rome.
2. Locate Philippi on the map and describe Paul's close relationship to the church in that city.
3. What was Paul's main purpose in writing this letter?
4. List several of Paul's references to the "joy" of the Christian life. What is the permanent value of his emphasis on joy?
5. What are the principal factors that make Paul's letters effective? What were his weaknesses as a writer?

CHAPTER ELEVEN: *Ephesians*

1. Read Ephesians, noting the devotional nature of the author's style.
2. Compare Ephesians and Colossians. Do you feel that the author of Ephesians has borrowed ideas from the earlier letter?
3. Read chs. 1:15 to 3:21 and briefly state the philosophy of history described in this passage.
4. List several ways in which the teaching of this book can be useful in the modern "ecumenical movement" of Christendom.
5. Write a paragraph explaining as precisely as possible what the author means by describing the church as "the body of Christ" (ch. 1:22–23).

CHAPTER TWELVE: *The Pastoral Letters*

1. Read the three pastoral letters, noting the similarities in style and content.

2. These letters were originally written to Christian "pastors." List several ways in which they are of value to pastors today. Are they of any value to laymen?

3. Record the key passages in which the author equates faith with "correct belief." How does this differ from Paul's conception of faith?

4. E. F. Scott, a prominent scholar, has made the following evaluation of the pastorals: "Yet with all their lack of deeper spiritual insight, the epistles teach a genuine Christianity, in some ways superior to the mystical fervor of Paul for the ordinary man." Do you agree? Defend your answer.

5. Write a brief essay on "The Ideal Minister" as described in these letters. Do you believe the author has really included the important aspects of the minister's life and work?

CHAPTER THIRTEEN: *Hebrews*

1. Read Hebrews, following carefully the author's *main argument*.

2. List four principal reasons why the majority of scholars now reject the Pauline authorship of this book. Give textual evidence where possible.

3. This author believes that Christianity is "the absolute religion." Do you agree? What is the relation of other religions to Christianity?

4. Read ch. 11. Define "faith" as understood by this author. Compare this definition with the concept of faith held by (a) Paul and (b) the author of the pastoral letters.

5. Using a good Bible dictionary, write a brief description of Jewish temple worship on the Day of Atonement, emphasizing the role of the priest and the sacrifice. Show how the argument of Hebrews is

closely related to this aspect of Jewish worship.

CHAPTER FOURTEEN: *The Gospel of Mark*

1. Read Mark, noting especially the tense dramatic style of presentation.
2. Read the first chapter of Mark and compare it with the parallel material in Matthew and Luke. As a result of your reading, list several of the most obvious differences between Mark and the other two Synoptic Gospels.
3. Using Mark's Gospel as a guide, make an outline of the ministry of Jesus.
4. List several reasons why Mark's Gospel seems to be earlier than the other three.
5. Read ch. 13. Does this sound like an authentic message of Jesus'? What is the permanent religious value of this chapter?

CHAPTER FIFTEEN: *The Gospel of Matthew*

1. Read Matthew, with special attention to his presentation of the teaching of Jesus.
2. Why does the author of Matthew quote the Old Testament so often? List several examples of this practice.
3. Read the Sermon on the Mount (chs. 5 to 7) and outline its main teachings.
4. Read ch. 16:13–20. What did Jesus mean when he said to Peter, "On this rock I will build my church"? How do you account for this statement's appearing only in Matthew?
5. List several characteristics of Matthew that make it well suited for the first position in the New Testament canon.

CHAPTER SIXTEEN: *The Gospel of Luke*

1. Read Luke, following the outline carefully in order

to observe Luke's additions to the record of Jesus' life and teaching.

2. Compare Luke, chs. 1 and 2, with Matthew 1:18 to 2:23. How do you account for the wide variance in the reports of Jesus' birth?

3. Read Luke, ch. 15. Why has Luke grouped these three parables together? What is the main teaching of the parable of the prodigal son?

4. List the passages in this Gospel that illustrate Luke's special interest in the prayer life of Jesus. Why don't the Gospels devote more time to this phase of Jesus' life?

5. Compare the Sermon on the Mount (Matt., chs. 5 to 7) with Luke's report of the same discourse (Luke, ch. 6). How do you account for the differences between the two?

CHAPTER SEVENTEEN: *The Acts of the Apostles*

1. Read The Acts, noting the author's special interest in Peter and Paul.

2. After reading The Acts, write a brief evaluation of Luke as a historian. Does he live up to the scholarly objectives stated in the preface to his work? (Luke 1:1–4).

3. List several passages in which Luke stresses the presence of the Holy Spirit in the life of the early church. What does he mean by the Holy Spirit? Why does he emphasize this concept so often?

4. Carefully compare the three accounts of the conversion of Paul (Acts, chs. 9;22;26). How do you account for the differences in these reports? What do they all have in common?

5. The book of The Acts describes the spread of Christianity from Jerusalem to Rome. What is the author's main purpose in telling this story?

CHAPTER EIGHTEEN: *First Peter*

1. Read First Peter, noting especially the way in which the author's style conveys a feeling of hope and courage.
2. What qualities and teachings in this letter would be helpful to you if you were a Christian suffering under Roman persecution?
3. This has been called the "epistle of hope." Justify this title, supporting your answer with passages from the text.
4. What are the main reasons for this author's firm hope? What is the permanent religious value of his teaching on this subject?
5. What is meant by the author's statement that Christ "went and preached to the spirits in prison" after his death (ch. 3:19)? Is this teaching accepted by modern Christians?

CHAPTER NINETEEN: *The Revelation to John*

1. Read The Revelation, looking especially for religious teaching of permanent value.
2. What qualities and teachings in this book would be helpful to you if you were a Christian suffering under Roman persecution?
3. State in your own words the message of the book of The Revelation.
4. List several reasons why modern Christians find the book of The Revelation confusing. What helpful principles can be used in the interpretation of it?
5. What is the greatest weakness of this book from the standpoint of modern Christianity? What is its greatest strength?

CHAPTER TWENTY: *James*

1. Read James, noting its strong moralistic tone.
2. List several passages in which the author attacks

wealth. How does this attitude compare with the teaching of Jesus on this subject?

3. It has often been said that the attitude of James is much closer to the Synoptic Gospels than any other book in the New Testament. What do you think is meant by this statement?
4. Evaluate James's definition of religion in ch. 1:27. Do you feel that it is adequate and accurate?
5. Read ch. 2:14–26 and then write a statement on the relation of faith and works in Christian experience.

CHAPTER TWENTY-ONE: *The Gospel of John*

1. Read John, noting the way in which the author departs from Mark's outline of the ministry of Jesus.
2. Read ch. 1:1–18 and state in your own words, as clearly as possible, the meaning of the concept of Jesus as the Word (Logos).
3. List several differences in John's portrait of Jesus as compared with that of the Synoptics.
4. The author of this Gospel has been called the "historian of the inner consciousness of Jesus." Defend this title, using passages from the text to support your answer.
5. In this Gospel, Jesus speaks more of "eternal life" than he does of the Kingdom of God. Precisely what did he mean by eternal life?

CHAPTER TWENTY-TWO: *The Letters of John*

1. Read the three letters of John, comparing the literary style with that of the Fourth Gospel.
2. Describe at least three ways in which Gnosticism attempted to pervert the true meaning of Christianity. You may want to use a Bible dictionary or encyclopedia of religion to enrich your answer.
3. What are the main arguments that this author uses in defending Christianity against Gnosticism?

4. It is often said that The First Letter of John is a necessary supplement to the Fourth Gospel. What is meant by this statement?

5. This author uses brotherly love as a test of religion (I John 4:7–21). Is this an adequate test? What are its limitations?

CHAPTER TWENTY-THREE: *Jude and Second Peter*

1. Read Jude and Second Peter, noting their close relationship.

2. What is the permanent religious value of these two short notes?

3. Why did the author of Second Peter feel it necessary to revive the teaching about the Second Coming of Christ?

CHAPTER TWENTY-FOUR: *The New Testament Canon*

1. Why was the early church slow in developing a scripture of its own?

2. What factors finally led the church to create a canon or "standard" collection of writings?

3. Describe the principal stages in the selection of a canon, from the earliest collections to the Easter letter of Athanasius.

4. What principles were used in the selection of writings for the New Testament canon?

5. Do you feel that other "inspired books" should be added to the New Testament canon?

The Church at the Close of the First Century